Soldier's Field

Log Line

An Hispanic boy, caught between his mother's
faith and his father's gang life, discovers after a
series of tragic events that love and
forgiveness free him to live a meaningful life.

Synopsis

Soldier's Field is a 37,500 word non-
fiction novel about a young Hispanic boy,
caught between his mother's faith and his
father's gang life, who discovers after a series
of tragic events that love and forgiveness free
him to live a meaningful life.

It's the 1980s in San Jose, California, a
hot battleground for rival gangs. Young Nacho
Pizano was raised by his mother, a woman of
remarkable faith and a strong work ethic.
When his father, a ruthless drug-using gang
member re-enters his life, Nacho is exposed to
life in the streets. Life at home spirals

downward and Nacho finds the acceptance he needs among the homeboys of 'La Ganga'. While he is rejected by his most members of his church and his public school teachers, some hold onto hope for Nacho, especially Mary, a girl about Nacho's age. When a church youth trip to Disneyland ends tragically with the death of everyone in the car (including Mary), Nacho beings to wonder if there is supposed to be a purpose to his life.

Street life takes over Nacho's life and he looses himself in "La Ganga," only to wind up in San Quentin Prison for a murder he doesn't recall committing. The youngest man sentenced to San Quentin, Nacho discovers the walls do not keep the gang life out; instead, it only condenses it. Again, Nacho wonders about the meaning and purpose of life while he is challenged to fight battles inside prison. In a strange twist of events, Nacho is released due to legal errors and his mother's unfailing love and faith. When his first son is born, Nacho realizes for the first time that his purpose is to break the pattern in which he was raised and to improve the lives of those around him.

        Soldier's Field is a biography of Nacho Pizano, a former dedicated member of a gang, who has used forgiveness to turn his life around and dedicated it to keeping at-risk children from entering the gang and drug lifestyle. Today, Nacho has an award-winning basketball team and has inspired numerous at-risk boys to go into college. Those who did so have expressed their gratitude to 'Coach Pizano', the man who opened his home, his life, and his heart to them. I have written this work because Nacho Pizano couldn't. With his limited education, he could only tell his story. As a veteran public educator of twenty-five years, I am familiar with the struggles of today's adolescents as they search for meaning and purpose in their lives. Nacho has spoken at numerous churches were the audience have requested a book about his life.

        Soldier's Field is a true story for those who want to be inspired by a story of struggle, faith, forgiveness, and hope.

Prologue

Forgiveness blossoms best in the evilest of soil- the worse the offense; the sweeter the forgiveness. Forgiveness is not a part of human nature, but the indwelling spark of the Divine urging us to love each other. It does not come easily for us to understand, nor is it easy to do. To forgive runs counter to humanity's innate instincts of guilt and revenge; yet, we are capable of forgiving because we first experienced forgiveness in our lives. Too often, people look upon the heartbreaking events in life caused by others as defining the pattern for their lives instead of an opportunity to grow from the experience. Robert Kennedy wrote "Tragedy is a tool for the living to gain wisdom, not a guide by which to live." Forgiveness is love's path to wisdom; it is not for the weak, but for the strong and courageous.

The world is filled with people seeking meaning and purpose in life, each person has a story to tell about their journey. This book is the story of one man's journey. It could easily be the story of many; however, this story is unique. Tragedies that would have crushed the human spirit and guided their lives, this man found wisdom, strength, and courage in the power of forgiveness to define his life's path. He had the word 'Forgiven' tattooed on his arm- covering the gang tattoos of his former life. It is a testimony to the power of forgiveness and the human will to seek peace and understanding.

I
Day and night

The pungent odors of stale smoke from cigarettes and marijuana merged with the rank stench from the toilets in the cellblock. As the boy sat on his bunk, he could feel the fear welling up inside him. His stomach quivered each time he heard the angry shouts of the other convicts as they challenged each other from behind their bars. Anger grows when it is all penned up inside and has no place to go. Swelling up inside each small cell, anger was feasting on the souls of those locked up. When it spilled out, the waves of foul language stank like the smoke and toilets. Even when the bars did not separate them, the convicts were imprisoned within their worlds of hate and distrust. Each man was a prison cell within himself- layered of frustration, guilt, and anger. The sounds bounced off the walls making the conversations difficult to follow.

"Marcello...Marcello. You did this to

me, Marcello. No, no…I did this to me. I let you do this to me," the boy thought to himself.

"Hey, man, you got a lenyo?" A raspy, disembodied voice from a nearby cell whispered as it cut through the sounds of the television and shouting interrupting his thoughts.

The boy thought if he didn't answer, perhaps the man wouldn't ask again.

"Weed? Weed, you got any? You can hear me, don't pretend you cain't."

"No, I just got here."
The boy was shocked to hear his own voice. It had betrayed his presence.

"Fish. Hey, y'all, we got a fish here," the man yelled out as some laughter echoed down the cellblock.

A distant voice responded, "Fish! I feel like fishin'."

"I got somethin' here for you little fish!"

That voice was closer, and the loud laughter that followed frightened the boy.

As the screaming threats and laughter a

few cells down grew louder, chills overtook the boy. The urge to puke became overwhelming. His mouth began to water, and the heaving began. Leaning over the toilet, his belly convulsed and the sour taste of undigested spaghetti filled his mouth. Somehow, the toilet seemed safe and familiar as he grasped the metal sides.

Fear has a scent.

He knew this, and the dread that the others would sense that in him crammed his thoughts. He could not be afraid, but fear was his only companion in this small cell. Shakily sliding back onto the bunk, his head pounded in pain as his belly cramped and convulsed. Like the shouts resounding in the cellblock, the acrid odor of the puke lingered.

"I gotta wash," he thought to himself. Attached to the toilet was a small steel sink and faucet. As he cupped his hands to catch the fresh water, he felt its cleanness and purity. Lowering his face into his hands, he ceremoniously splashed it onto his face and felt the gentle tingle of its coolness. How he wished he could wash himself of this place. Caught in the moment of washing, his memories flooded.

"Mico, wash your face and hands." His mother's voice came back to him. "Did you use soap?"

Tears welled up in his eyes. He grabbed the towel and patted his face dry. The flash of reprieve refreshed him, but the filthy reality of the place slapped him. His eyes, still smarting from the tears, darted across the small cell. This was his world. The mustard yellow walls matched the odor of the stale urine in the cellblock. The cacophony of men talking, bars clanging, and toilets flushing interrupted the drone of the televisions. It all seemed so unreal.

"How small is this cell," he wondered as he tried to measure his new world. As the fingertips of one hand touched the far wall, his elbow on this other arm touched the other wall- about 4 and a half feet. The reality that he couldn't stretch his arms out full-length struck him that the boundaries of this place were intended to invade his personal space. There was no personal space in this world as the walls, sights, sounds and smells were totally invasive, corrupting every bit of individuality. There was no privacy except in his mind, and these were never to be shared with anyone. Weak people share their thoughts and emotions. Weak people die in here; that is, if they haven't already died inside…deep inside.

A roaring sound of water splashing into a metal tank resounded from the cell next to his. The raspy-voiced man was taking a leak. The man farted, and made the sound of satisfaction. Real men fart and grunt- a grunt of pleasure is the animal in the man. There is a thin veil between man and animal, and this new world of his showed the boy that the veil disappears.

"Lights out!"

As the cellblock began to dim, he looked at the white bars of the door to his cell. Chipped paint revealed that the bars had been painted many times, each time the paint had failed to stick in spots. Like life, each fresh coat becomes worn- revealing the ugly underneath. Some things are never covered, only temporarily masked.

Staring at the bars he wondered, "How can life be made clean? Maybe the morning will provide a fresh start."

Sleep came, but only as short moments punctuated by the night sounds. It was a night that seemed endless. The threats, swearing, and toilets flushing broke what little silence there was. "Hey man, can I catch a ride?" a voice whispered. "Yeah, here." another answered back. Soon, the sweet aroma of weed wafted by his cell, and his dreams were disjointed and out of order. "Stupid, stupid," he thought as he tried to make sense of his random thoughts. Nothing made sense, nothing. Time was meaningless.

Morning comes early in San Quentin prison. By 5 am, he was in the 'work line' on his way to making cheese sandwiches in the sandwich room. The oily cheese slices coated his fingertips, making them feel greasy and dirty. It became a foggy, mindless activity and, as tired as he was, time passed slowly. His thoughts drifted back to eating cheese sandwiches for lunch at his elementary school. School held few fond memories for the boy. He couldn't remember the names of the teachers, and he doubted they remembered him either. They seemed like faceless figures with lives of their own in the grey cold world of school. As he thought back, he recalled only a few school days in San Jose when the sun seemed to shine.

"C'mon, hurry up Nacho! We're on a schedule. Snap to it!" The bull-voice of the guard bellowed out with annoyance at the boy's lack of speed. 'Nacho', to hear his name reminded him that he was someone. 'Nacho'. His mother used to call him that as she woke him up in the mornings when he was little. 'Nacho' or, when she spoke to him in love it was 'Mico'. The sudden thought of his mother saddened him for a moment. What was his mother doing right now? Was she making breakfast? Was she thinking about him?

"Nacho, did you hear me? Speed it up!

It's almost 7. Move it!"

As the boy looked around, he saw a thin, wiry man giving him the 'red eye' hard stare. "Yo, Chico…Chico…you hear me, Chico? You're mine." A few of the men chuckled when they heard the threat, but kept their heads down. The boy knew what that meant. He'd heard the word before, when he was on the streets. 'Chico' is the enemy gang's term for their rivals, La Ganga. Somehow, he'd been identified as a member of the La Gangas-a Homeboy- and he was now a target.

"Line up. Time for breakfast. Line up!" The guard's voice broke the moment- broke the fear. As they lined up, the 'red eye' man whispered to the boy, "The chotas can't help you. Remember that. Look down. Look down. Don't look at me. Don't look up. You ain't worth nothin'." He knew the 'red eye' man was right, the guards couldn't help him. No one could. He was on his own. But, he was something. He was. Down deep, he knew he was. He was worth something.

As they made their way to the chow hall,

he saw that breakfast was powdered eggs and milk. As he looked for a place to sit, he knew he'd have to be careful. One table was empty, and he headed for it. It wasn't long, though, before several others were at the table with him. The chalky tasting eggs were runny. A few small bites were all he could choke down.

"Time to 'jug up'." As he quickly glanced to see who spoke, he saw a white man across from him. He seemed to be fortyish, with thinning hair. His left hand was scarred and mottled. His nails were bitten down to a nub; yet, they still looked dirty.

"Scott"

"Huh?"

"My name is Scott."

"Oh, yeah. Nacho."

Just as Nacho got ready to say more, the man suddenly appeared uncomfortable as another sat down to the right of Nacho. This man's hands were big, almost unnaturally so. He was big, and his size suddenly made Nacho feel small. Words did not need to be spoken. This man had a presence of power and respect that came from inside the walls of prison. They were soon joined by another who, as he sat to Nacho's left, cleared his throat. Without looking up from his breakfast, Nacho's could see that the third man was of medium build, but muscular. Both of the men were Hispanic. Nacho leaned back for a moment to catch his breath. As he did so, the white man's eyes widened as if being threatened by Nacho's movement. He quickly shoved his food into his mouth and had nothing more to say.

"Hey, Bro."

Nacho glanced to his left, and saw the man looking at him expecting a response.

"Hey."

The big man just sat, examining Nacho behind an expressionless face.

"Don't have much to say, eh, Bro?"

"Not much."

"Hmmm. Man don't have much to say."

Scott, shoveled the last of his breakfast into his mouth without looking up. As he rose to leave, the big man shifted in his seat.

The big man took a bite of his breakfast, but

didn't stop staring at Nacho. He didn't speak, either.

"What 'cha' in for?"

Nacho thought for a moment. Should he share?

"Murder."

As he said the word, he realized its significance. He had ended a man's life. By doing that, he was a murderer. But the cost was his life, too. Not one man died that day, but two. He was also a victim of his crime, and now he had to pay up.

"Murder, huh? " There was a silence at the table, and as Nacho looked up he saw the big man nod slightly, but his face was like a rock-no emotion- just a stare of evaluation.

"Scott ain't worth knowin."

"Who?"

"The guy you was talkin' to 'fore we came. He ain't worth knowin'. He's a 'chester'. Stay away from him."

"A chester?" Nacho wasn't up on that term.

"Man, a 'chester'," he said with disgust

at Nacho's ignorance, "you know, he likes little children. That's why he's here. He raped a boy and damn near killed him. He's a 'chester'. You see his hands? One day ol' Scott found his hand shoved into some boiling water, he did. Don't be talkin' to no 'chesters'."

Nacho saw the large mural on the wall of the chow hall, and wondered why he hadn't looked at it the night before. He looked down at his plate and saw the scrambled eggs. Their appearance sickened him. He'd had enough. As he returned to his cell, he settled back on his bunk. The night had been rough, but he'd known worse. His mind began to drift back to when he was a kid. Life seemed easier then.

II
Mico's Morning

It was a hot Saturday morning in San Jose, California, "with temperatures expected to be in the low 90s." At least, that is what the weatherman had said on the radio the night before. As the warm summer breeze fluttered into the open window, the sleepy boy awoke and lay there with his hands cradling his head, staring at the ceiling as the morning glow splashed across the room.

"Mico, are you awake?" His mother always called him 'Mico', short for 'mi corazon' or 'my heart'.

"Mmm."

"I have to go to work. You know what you're supposed to do?"

"Mmmm."

"C'mon, son, it's time to get up. Wash your face and come out for breakfast."

"Mmmm."

"Did you hear me? C'mon...time to get up!"

The warm scent of the summer breeze

carried with it the sweet aroma of freshly cut grass. As he slowly crawled out of bed, he looked around his small room. The door to the outside was the half of a closet door near the head of his bed. Tied shut, it was usually covered with a piece of plastic tarp during the winter to keep the cold at bay. Now that it was summer, the tarp had been removed. His Levis were lying in the closet at the foot of his bed where he left them the night before. Wrinkled and worn, they were comfortable from use. As he slipped the Levis on, his little toe was caught in a hole in the pocket. The more he pushed, the more the Levi's held his toe.

"Estúpido."

He pulled his toe out of the hole, and wiggled his foot through the pant leg.
He found a tee shirt jammed in the corner, slipped it over his head, and opened the bedroom door. His mother had cleaned the house the evening before, and the small house still smelled of Pine-Sol. His day began like all other days before it.   He found some tortillas from the night before, and stuffed them slowly

into his mouth. Taking a swig of lukewarm water from a glass on the kitchen counter, he munched on them until he made a cornmeal and water slurry. The gritty feel of the corn mush on his tongue was a simple pleasure, like many of the simple pleasures he had.

"Everybody's headin' for McDonald's land. Hurry in and scurry in to McDonald's Land..." The television commercial attracted his attention for a second, as the dancing clown and other characters mesmerized the boy. Standing in front of the small black and white screen by the fireplace, his expression was without emotion. He stood there, frozen, staring at the screen until the commercial was completed, then flicked off the television. In the distance, he heard the familiar repetitious 'chick, chick, chick, chit, chat, chat, chat chat' of the neighbor's sprinkler. Somewhere in another yard, a bird was chirping.

"Mico! Mico!"

"Hmm?"

"I'm going now, Mico. I'll be back later. You know what today is?"

"Hmmm?"

"Its Friday!"

"Oh, yeah. Friday."

Fridays were special for the boy and his mother. Payday, Fridays were the one day of the week when they would go out to Arby's for a beef sandwich. His mother always took a couple of pieces of extra bread along, and they would split the meat of the one sandwich she would buy between them.

"Something to look forward to, Mico, Si?"

"Si, es bueno!"

He stood by the door and watched as his mother walked down the street to the bus stop. Taking one last look around the house, he leapt out of the front door and ran to the small patch of dried grass and dirt by the garage in front of the house. The dirty wood clothespins that were his toy cars and people were strewn about with abandon. He stood there carefully examining his toys. Something was not right. The road he carved in the dried dirt the day before seemed different somehow. A fly landed on his right arm and he swatted at it with no intention of killing it, but to merely move it along its way. Doing so, he noticed the fly didn't move. It remained, perched on his forearm. As his left hand slapped down to smash the insect, he felt its small trapped body buzzing between his fingers. Anger welled up inside Mico's little body as he tightened his grip. He felt an ever-so-slight snap and splash of moisture as the fly's movement ceased. He took the crushed body to the sidewalk and smeared it with his barefoot so that only fragments of insect parts and moisture remained.

Morning became noon, and Mico shrugged off the urge to eat. His play swallowed his time. Black, thick ropes, moist with sweat and dirt, formed around the back of his neck. The dust of his roads clung to his face and arms while he gritted his teeth, hummed, and made the sounds of truck gears shifting. These were big trucks doing man's work.

"Hey." It was the black boy from down the street, Tony. About a year older than Mico, he lived with his mom and 'uncle'. He had lots of 'uncles', it seemed to Mico, and none of them ever gave Tony much attention.

"Hey, whatch'a doin'?"

"Playin'."

"Wanna play ball? I gots me a ball. I found it down by the end of the schoolyard. It's a football, but it's kinda flat."

"Sure!"

Within minutes, several other children joined Mico and Tony on Biscane Way, and the street was echoing with the shouts and yells of youth. Tony's best friend was Frankie. They were tight- like brothers. Mico knew this, and wished he had a friend who could be that close, but he couldn't find that kind of friendship. Tony and Frankie were always doing things together, like riding bikes, sharing candy bars, and stuff like that. They had secrets. They had jokes only the two of them shared. They were always together. Frankie's younger brother, Jaime, was always trying to hang around his older brother. Jaime was a good kid, but didn't show much sense. He was always doing stupid things, trying to prove himself to Frankie and Tony. One day, Jaime threw a knife into the air to show that he could catch it. Thing was, the knife landed in Jaime's eye. He lost the eye and had a scar on his cheek. The only one who looked up to Jaime was Carlos, Frankie and Jaime's five year old brother. He was a small kid, with big ears and eyes like a mouse.

"Yo, little bro, get yo ass off the street! You get it runned over, little man."
One of Tony's 'uncles' came driving up slowly with several others.
"There ain't enuf to run over on that kid, Corky," one of them said. "Look at him! He's a squirrel, man, a little squirrel. Run, squirrel!" With that, the man jumped out of the car and started chasing Mico. The faster he ran, the slower it seemed he was. His feet felt like they were weighted down, and he felt the tears welling up in his eyes. Why was this guy chasing him? As the other children watched Mico run, they started laughing. "Nacho, he's catching up to ya! Run, Nacho, run faster!"

All of the kids called Mico "Nacho." Nacho was short for his full name, Ignacio. But in his mind, he called himself "Mico." Nacho was the name others called him.

He could hear the footfalls of someone behind him. The closer they got, the more Mico felt fear. Looking around, Mico saw another car drive slowly past. A quick glance at the car is all Mico could manage, but what he saw looked like the devil. A mean, dark face glared at him with eyes that were piercing and sharp and a lower jaw that jutted out. Mico's heart was pounding and his ribs began to hurt from the deep breaths. As suddenly as it had started, the chase stopped as the slap-slap of the shoes behind him fell silent. Risking a quick glance, he saw he was no longer the prey. Far behind him, he could see a man walking back to Tony's house- back to a waiting car- the sounds of laughter fell silent. As the sound of a distant plane whined above him, he wished he could fly- fly from this place of fear, of pain, of anger. As he slowly made his way home, loneliness filled him. As he sat to catch his breath, he looked around him and saw the familiar neighborhood with the parked cars. In one of them, across the street from Mico's house, sat the man with the 'devil's face' talking to the driver of the car. As the car started to drive away slowly, the man gave Mico a second glance. As Mico made his way back into the safety of his home, he passed his toys scattered in the dirt. It seemed like hours passed until his mother returned home from work.

"Mico! Mico, I'm home! Are you ready to go for dinner?" His mother's voice carried the warmth of love.

"I'm in here, in the bathroom!"

"C'mon, Mico, I'm hungry. How was your day? Did you have fun?" His mother's questions poured from her with concern. He was her life, her love, her heart. Walking out of the bathroom, he saw the tired and worn face of his mother light up as she glanced at him. As she hugged him, he could smell the scent of the cannery on her- tomatoes and sweat. She already packed the extra pieces of bread in her purse to make a second sandwich from the meat of the one sandwich she would buy. She always did that-split the sandwich meat to make two, making sure that Mico had more meat than she did.

Their trip to Arby's was always something to enjoy. It was their time together- time to relax and talk about what mattered most- their love for each other, life, and faith. Mico's mother was a woman of faith, and she loved to share stories about how Jesus watched over and blessed them. She spoke of God's love, and how He loves his children always. As Mico listened, he recalled his day and wondered why it was that his life didn't seem to fit that.

"If God loves me, why do I feel scared sometimes? Why do I want to beat some of those guys into a bloody mess? Why do my friends invite me to join them in playing, but don't stick up for me when I am being chased?" Mico's questions weren't spoken, but were held deep inside with the myriad of other questions he had about life, love, God, and himself.

III

The Devil Comes In Many Ways

The air was cool; gathering clouds promised a winter rain. The empty schoolyard was a great place to play on a Saturday afternoon. A bunch of kids were playing basketball, and Mico was among them. He had a way with playing basketball; some might call it 'a gift'. He loved the game and even though he was six, it seemed like he could get lost in it. Tony, Frankie, and Jamie were out there tossing the ball, dribbling, and making a few good shots while whistling the 'Harlem Globetrotters Sweet Georgia Brown' song. It was one of those days that it seemed like nothing could go wrong.

"I'm going home, but I'll be back in a few minutes," Mico shouted to his friends. "What? If you have to take a piss go over there by the building," Jaime shouted accompanied by laughter from some of the other boys.

"No, that's not it. It's the other business, and I'm not doing that here!" The laughter increased, as the boys started making grunting noises.

"I NEED to go. 'Sides, I don't want no skid marks on my pants."

"Well then, Nacho, make it fast 'cause we don't got all day."

"It won't take too long, I promise," he said running towards home. When he got there, he saw his sister's car in front of the house. Rachel, Mico's half-sister, was about twenty years older than him.

"What's HE doing here?" Rachel's voice sounded angry. As Mico opened the door, he could sense the tension in the room. His mother was standing by the fireplace. Rachel was near her, and in the chair sat a man. It was HIM- the man with the "Devil's face." He sat motionless, staring at the fireplace.

"Mico, this is your father."
Mico came up to see the man, but the man made no effort to acknowledge Mico's presence. Instead, he stared at Mico with those sharp, piercing eyes.   Mico waited.

"Maybe he'll hug me. I hope so,"

thought Mico, "after all, isn't that what fathers do?" Mico waited, but no hug was there. Instead, the man sat in the chair and stared at Mico. The man had tattoos that covered his arms. He smelled of dirt, sweat, and cigarettes. His jutting jaw gave him a mean look. There was no love in the man's eyes, only emptiness.

"Rachel, Ignacio needs a dad. I am not going to argue with you. Marcello is his dad, and he needs his dad."

"I don't understand you. I just don't understand you! Don't you see what he is? Is this what you want for Nacho? Mom, he's just a little boy."

"I'm through talking about this, Rachel. Do you hear me? I am through!"

"I can't believe this. There ought to be a law or something."

As Mico looked at the man- his father- the man turned his head and stared at Mico. Mico started to feel scared.

"Come here," his dad said. Mico took a step forward. His dad leaned forward a bit and made a snorting sound.

"Mico, your dad is moving in with us so we can be a family."

When his mother said this, Mico knew life would never be the same. The home would not be same. Rachel wouldn't let go of it, and kept arguing with her mother.

"Nacho doesn't need this!"

"Nacho is my concern, Rachel. Marcello is going to live here. That is final!"

"What's final is you are giving Nacho up. Mom, seriously? You really think this is good? That man will take over Nacho's life and run him to the ground. He'll run him to the ground just he did you and himself."

While they argued, Mico's dad lifted his finger slightly and pointed at Mico.

"I saw you runnin'," his dad whispered, "runnin'. No son of mine runs from nothin'. You ain't nothin', so stay clear of me. You understand? I see you runnin' from somebody, I'll beat you so you wish you hadn't been borned."

There was a silence.

Rachel was not going to give up her argument. "Is this what you want for him? You want him like this? With this...this man, if that's what you want to call him?"

Rachel's anger was rising, and Marcello gave her a look like a shot from hell.

"Listen, little girl, this ain't none of your business. I am here to raise my son to be a man. Your mom asked me to come here and get him to be a man. So, a door is there...use it."

Mico stood still, wide-eyed and holding his breath as his legs became weak with fear. His dad sat back and reached in his pocket for his cigarettes. The slam of the front door shook Mico from his trance.

Rachel left.

As the months passed, Mico's days were filled with school and playing with his friends. Getting up early, he had to be quiet so as not to disturb his dad who was sleeping off a night of being out drinking and doing drugs.

His mother had changed since his dad moved in, and Mico was left to care for himself. There were times when she would still take Mico out to Arby's, to the store, or to church, but those were short times -too short- too brief. The schoolyard and classroom were cold and unwelcoming. His teachers seemed to care little for him, and he began to sense that he was 'outside'. The classroom walls were decorated for Halloween, then Thanksgiving, and finally Christmas. As much as the decorations changed showing the passing of the seasons and holidays, Mico's life remained one of solitary struggle.

"What's the matter with you? Can't you do anything right? You stupid   bitch!" Mico awoke with a start. It was early morning. The sun had hardly come up over the hills. It was Mico's dad yelling at his mother again. It seemed like all they did was argue. Quietly, he slipped out of bed and walked to the bedroom door to listen. The room was cold and dark, and the voices were as cold and sharp as the draft that blew through the poorly sealed closet door that went from his room into the backyard.

"Marcello, stop it. Please, no. I'm sorry. I'll do better next time," he heard his mother say in a quiet voice.

SLAP! SLAP!

"I'll do better, really," she cried.

Mico knew his mom was being hit, but what could he do? As he slowly opened the door to peek out, his dad shot a look in his direction. "Back in your room or I'll give you some of the same, you little bastard!" Jumping back, he covered his head with his thin blanket half expecting his dad to beat him. As he lay there, he wished he could go back to before his dad came home.

The next morning, Mico quietly crept from his room. His dad was asleep on the chair. He awoke and through glazed eyes looked at Mico.

"Get me some water." Mico slipped into the kitchen and grabbed a glass of water for him. Handing it to him, he noticed a needle on the floor. He'd been 'shooting up'.

"Cold water, stupid. Can't you do

nothing right?" his father bellowed. His father slammed the glass on the table beside the chair, spilling some of it on the chair. Suddenly, his father smacked him across the face with an open hand. The sting on his cheek sent him reeling. His head spun, and he tasted blood in his mouth. He had bit his tongue, and the metalic taste of blood filled his mouth. "Ow! I'm sorry. I didn't mean to...," but his words were cut short by his father's swearing.

"Here, Marcello. Here is some water for you." It was his mother's voice behind him. "Marcello, please calm down. He's just a boy. I'm going to church. Mico, go with me. Grab some breakfast, and be quick." His mother always wanted Mico to attend church. A woman of faith, Mico's mother wanted that for Mico as well.

"Is dad coming with us?"

"No, Mico. It will just be the two of us." Mico stuffed some tortillas and left over beans from the night before into his mouth, being careful not to bite his swollen tongue. As he washed his face, he checked where he had chomped down on his tongue. The bleeding hadn't stopped, and the sting was still there. His tongue was swollen, and his face was red where he had been slapped. "Why IS he here?" Mico wondered. Had he done something wrong? Was his mother punishing him for something?

The church was decorated for Christmas, even though it was still several weeks away. Some of the kids were talking in a small group and, when Mico walked in, their voices were lowered as they gave him a fleeting look. Their whispers betrayed their feelings, and Mico knew they were talking about him. He took a cautious step towards them, but they moved away from him as if to avoid him.

"That's Marcello's kid," one woman said to another as if Mico wasn't there. "Hmm, like his dad I suppose," the other woman responded, "kinda looks like him. Pizano...bad seed."

As he looked down at his beat up shoes,

Mico felt that all eyes were on him. An overwhelming dread washed over him as he walked next to his mother.   "Are we going to stay long, Mom?"

"Mico, we're here to worship. We'll be here for about an hour or so. Why? What's the matter? You have someplace to be?"

Mico shook his head, resigned to the fact that he was here to be judged. They took their seats and the worship began, but Mico felt like everyone was looking at him. The little church was a house with chairs and a small stage. The singing bounced against the walls making the small structure shake. When he looked around, he saw only one person was looking at him- a girl about his age. Her eyes were gentle, kind, and caring. She smiled at him, and he smiled back. His cheek, sore and swollen, made it hurt to smile; yet, he managed. His mother nudged him. "Listen to the pastor." He took one last peek at the girl who was no longer looking at him, and he wondered who she was. After the service, he saw her again. She was standing by a window waiting for her parents. As Mico approached, she looked at him and smiled.

"Hi, I'm Mary."

"Hey, I'm Nacho. So, umm, how are you?" She giggled. "I'm fine. You?"

"Fine." Come to think of it, he was. Comforted by the knowledge that he found someone who could be a friend at church, he did feel fine.

IV

School: Stay away; get an 'A'

"Pizano? Ignacio Pizano?"

"I like to be called Nacho"

"Whatever. You're present obviously."

"Yeah, present"

Some of the students giggled.

Classrooms have a smell, a smell of crayons and paper, pencils and books. This room had that smell plus the sweet perfume odor of some potpourri in a bowl on the teacher's desk. On the walls were posters with trite sayings: "It's attitude that matters," "Be Prepared- Be the Person You Want to Be," and "An 'A' is the Way." Some of the students' work was stapled to the wall in an obvious demonstration of excellent work, but Nacho never saw any of his papers on the wall. The best students received the praise; the others received little recognition. Nacho sat at a desk that showed wear from past students. The carvings on the desktop were the evidence that others had been there. It was their way of letting others know that they, too, had been there. He wondered who they were and what had happened to them. Did they pass their days like he did? The gum under the desk had hardened, and sometimes Nacho would pick at them mindlessly with his fingers.

The teacher's look of disgust cheered Nacho. He hated school. He hated teachers. In fact, the whole thing was a waste of time, and the teacher's sarcasm confirmed his attitude.

"Naw-chow," the teacher said mockingly," Nah-chow." Now that we know you're 'present-hay', could you tell me if you're 'red-day' to learn, or just be entertaining?"

"Whoa," one of the students said as Nacho glared at the teacher.

The teacher was challenging Nacho to respond. It became a stare-down, and Nacho looked at her with eyes dark and spiteful. He knew if he responded, he would be sent to the office. She would win the battle. After all, she didn't want him there anyways. The stare down lasted what seemed to be minutes, even though it was probably seconds. Neither side gave. The teacher finally turned away and started the lesson.

"Psst, Nacho…Nacho," a boy whispered. "Hey, pass this to Carla." It was a note, tightly folded with a crudely drawn heart on the top. Giving a fleeting look at the teacher, Nacho snatched the note and tossed it to Carla who caught it and placed it under her worn Pee Chee folder. Carla was a pretty girl with black hair that smelled like berries. Her parents had moved to San Jose from New Mexico a few years back, and her manners showed that her parents had money. From the corner of his eye, Nacho looked at the ochre folder with its drawings of basketball and baseball players. "Hmph, white kids playing," he thought to himself, "never see no kids like me on there." He looked out the window and wished he was outside. The teacher was talking. Kids around him were looking at their books and turning pages. In the back of the room, he could hear the clock ticking away the minutes. He yawned, and waited for something to happen that could stir his interest. A large fly, trying to find an exit from the room, occasionally went to the window and crawled along the glass. Its escape was as futile as Nacho's. The sharp buzz of the fly on the window was annoying to the teacher who casually walked over and crushed it with a piece of tissue.

"EEeewww!" some girls shrieked. "Did you get it?" one boy asked.

"Now that your little friend is gone are you going to pay attention Nacho?"
A few students giggled. The teacher rolled the crushed body into the tissue, forming a ball. As she tossed it into the large plastic wastepaper basket by her desk, the bell rang for recess.

Enrique, or 'Ricky' was already on the court with a basketball when Nacho got there.

"When are you gonna come by and play at my house?" Ricky asked.

"Maybe today. I dunno. Why?"

"Oh, nothin'. I got something I thought you'd like, that's all."

"Are we gonna talk or play?" It was Carlos, a lanky kid in another class. He always had bad breath, and the other kids would tease him about that. Carlos had just moved to San Jose from Sunnyvale, and the other kids heard that his older brother was killed in a driveby. The family moved to get away from the gangs, but some said that his dad was in deep.

"Hey, Carlos. We're just talkin' for a minute. C'mon, let's see how tough   you are, Chico."

Soon, the boys were playing. It was good to be outside having fun. The fresh, cool air felt good on their faces. For Nacho, this was the best –friends, fun, and the recognition that the mattered. Here was significance. Here was family.

As the rest of the day plodded along uneventfully, Nacho began to realize that his life was not in school, but with his friends. It was with his friends that he felt that he was wanted, needed… And yes even loved. At the end of the school day, as the students were putting their books away, his teacher told him to stay after because she wanted to talk to him. Nacho figured it had something to do with his grades. After all, he wasn't a good student. "Nacho, I need to talk to you. I know you don't like school and you don't like me, so I'll make you a deal. Just stay away from my classroom and I'll give you an 'A'. That way, I can teach, you can do what ever it is that you do and we will both be happy."

Nacho thought for a few moments. So this is what it was all about? A deal? If he stayed away, his teacher would give him an 'A'?

Nacho turned to leave. As he did so, he stopped for a moment and looked the classroom. Maybe this wasn't for him. He looked back at the teacher, who was looking out the large window," Hmmm, let me think about it." When he said that he noticed the teacher wasn't even turning to look at him. Slowly, he made his way to the door, opened it, and walked into the hall. "I'm not really wanted. In fact, I'm not really liked. My friends like me, but no one else does. Well, what does it matter?"

Walking home, he saw a familiar car parked in front. His slow footfalls sped, and he knew the day was going to better. Johnny was there. Nacho's older half-brother, Johnny was twenty-one. His height of over six feet and heavy build made him look formidable; yet, he was a gentle giant of a man, with a quick smile and warm embrace for everyone. Nacho always looked forward to Johnny's weekly visits when they would get the chance to go out and just be together. This day would be a good one.

"Hey, Nacho!" The familiar voice was friendly and welcoming as he entered the house. Johnny was a kind-hearted young man with a wisdom seldom found in men as young as he was. Nacho felt good about him, and he felt good about himself when he was with him. Nacho began to explain to Johnny what the teacher had said about not going to school, but Johnny stopped him. "Listen, Nacho, your education is important. You need to get out of this neighborhood. Life begins outside of this neighborhood. What keeps these people here together is the 'hood'. They can't accept change in the hood, so they fight to keep it together. They fight to keep things the way they've always been and they are caught in a trap that they made for themselves. They can't accept the change. That is why they can't grow. So listen, Nacho, your education is the most important thing for you."

"School? School ain't nothing. Why, you ain't even good at it, so why would you stay with it?" Nacho's father said in a low voice. "All you do is run from stuff, kid. You ain't nothin'…nothin'."

"Hey, the fact is he is good, Marcello." It was Johnny's voice, and there was a tone of defiance in it. "Fact is, Marcello, Nacho has brains and he's smart. He is smarter than anyone in here. Smarter than me, even. Smarter than you, I can tell you."

Marcello shot a quick look over at Johnny, then looked away. He muttered something quietly to himself.

"Yeah, you keep mumblin' to yourself,

Marcello. Yous' ta only one who'll listen to your stupidity."

Marcello made a motion like he was getting up from his chair, but he must have thought twice as Johnny took a step towards him.

"C'mon, Nacho, let's go."

As Nacho and Johnny walked out to the car, they could hear Marcello saying something.

"Ignore him. Its best to ignore him."

"Yeah, but I live here. Johnny, it isn't easy being here. Mom is tough, but he's tougher. He has some kinda hold on her and I…I don't know what it is."

"I know, man, I know. Some things in life are difficult to understand, like love n' such. Just know that your mom loves you."

"Yeah, I know. But, does she love him more? I figure if he is here, and she sees what is happening here, she don't care much about what's happening to me. Even Rachel sees it, Johnny. He is mean and full of hate, n' drugs, n' booze. I hate him. I really hate him. He don't even try to know me. I'm nothin' to him but trash in the house, Johnny. I hate him."

"Don't never say you hate anyone, Mico. I'm serious, little man. Hatin' like that don' make you no better than him. Makes you worse, even. You hatin' him means he got control of you. His hate is growing inside you like some kind cancer or something. Once it gets hold of you, there ain't no gettiin' rid of it. It'll grow and eat at you. No, Nacho, never say that. Just figure you better than him...better'n all of them. You'll see, someday you'll be a big man and make that hate into nothin' but dirt."

Nacho was silent. He was thinking about what Johnny said about hate. It was true, all that hate just boiled up inside him and made him feel bad, but it didn't do anything to his father. Fact was, maybe all that hate was just making' his father proud that he could fertilize hatred inside him and make him turn out like his dad.

"You sure got quiet, Nacho. Somethin' I said?"

"Yeah...well. Just that thing you said

about hate. Why he be hatin' so much? Why does he hate me n' mom n' Rachel n' you? Why didn't do nothin' to him to make him hate us so much. I don't even know the guy, and he hates me. It just don't seem right to be hatin' like that for no reason at all."

"Hate don't need a reason, Nacho. Hate just is what it is- evil. Once, Marcello was a kid just like you n' me. Once, he was a baby who couldn't do nothin' but eat n' sleep. Don't seem to me like he changed much there, though," Johnny said with a chuckle. Nacho started laughing too, just the thought of his dad being like a big baby that never grew up to be much of a man. After all, that just about summed up Marcello..eating and sleeping.

"Still, why'd he turn out that way? Something must've filled him up with hate, Johnny."

"Well, way I figure it, hate comes from anger n' anger comes from frustration n' frustration comes from not having enough love and opportunities to show love."

"Huh?" That was a bit too much for

Nacho to figure out, and he was getting hungry.

"I lost you on that, didn't I? I'm trying to figure it all out myself, too, Nacho. Hungry?"

It was like Johnny had read his mind. "Yeah, a bit. School sucked today. The teacher told me to stay away and she'd let me pass the class."

"No, that ain't right, Nacho. You know that ain't right. The teacher is just scared, that's all."

"Scared? Scared of what? I didn't do nothing wrong. I just sit there and think."

"That's what the teacher is probably scared of," Johnny said. "Probably you weren't thinking what she wanted you to think. That, or you got a reputation. Either way, it ain't right. You go to school."

"Johnny, you're smart. You know that? You're smart. Someday, I hope I'll be as smart as you are."

"Smart? Me?" Johnny started laughing. "Man, you must be hungry. You're going all weird on me. How about some snack? I got to get some gas, so we'll grab some cookies or something in the market while we're there."

As they pulled up to the gas station, Nacho thought how great it was to be hanging out with Johnny. Johnny knew things. He was smart, even though he didn't think so. Johnny had a way of making things seem better. They got the car gassed up, and Johnny bought a small snack size package of cookies for Nacho in the gas station market. The day was turning out to be good after all. Johnny was right.

Two weeks later, Johnny was dead. Nacho was, again, alone.

"It should have been you, you little...," Marcello had Nacho by the throat screaming. "Why do the good one's die, and the little jerks like you live. You're worthless, you know that?!" Nacho felt the life being chocked out of him, and his throat was closing up. As tears started rolling down Nacho's cheecks, Marcello started screaming even louder, but the words were drowned out by Nacho's fear. His mother was crying, screaming, and the whole world seemed to be closing in on him.

"Johnny...my Johnny," was all Nacho could hear from his mother as Marcello kept screaming. Spit was flying into Nacho's face, and the rancid odor of tobacco and alcohol from his father's breath splashed into his face. "You know something, you ain't worth nothin', nothin' to me. Why, you been costing me all your life you little piece of worthless..." Nacho struggled to get away, and finally managed to push his father away. Crying, he ran to his bedroom door and slammed it shut.

"I hate him. I hate him. I hate him," Nacho repeated over and over. Hate filled Nacho, and hate grew into anger; anger grew into rage. A furious rage overcame him. "When I die, when I die, I am going to die like a man. LIKE A MAN, YOU HEAR THAT!," Nacho screamed, but his screams of rage were drowned out by the sounds of yelling in the other room.

Nacho waited. He waited and listened to the dying sounds in the other room. "Someday,

someday that ol' man is going to die. I will do it. I will. Nobody ain't never going to treat me like that."

V

Days and Nights

"Yo, bro! Tonight, we gonna have some weed. You comin' over, or not?" Jaime's voice was hoarse.

"Vato, you got a cold or somethin? Your voice is, like, whacked. Yeah, I comin' over tonight," Nacho said, mimicking Jaime's hoarseness.

"We got a little somethin' to do first, then we meet over at my place. You wanna come along for the ride? We gots some guys who've got a need, and we got to drop some stuff off for them first," Jaime told Nacho as he wiped sweat from around his lips.

"Cool, sounds good to me."

As the two walked down the street talking, a car slowly drove by. The car windows were down, and as Nacho looked over he could see the driver had a bandana on. His dark glasses covered his eyes, and Nacho couldn't see if he was looking at him or at Jaime. The guy in the backseat had his hand hanging out of the window, and was banging a pistol on the side of the door.

"Hey, look at the Busters! Big bad busters, are you?," one of the passengers yelled out of the car.

"You wanna find out? C'mon, Esse! C'mon!" Nacho reached under his shirt, pulled out a Taurus 9 mm, and waved it in the air. The car stopped suddenly, and then peeled out down the road leaving tire smoke in the air.

"C'mon! You runnin?, " Nacho yelled out at the car as it sped away. Jaime stared at Nacho for a moment. "Man. You are crazy, vato.Crazy."

"When I die, I am going down like a soldier. I am going down wearing my colors. I don't care what they say, I'm going to wear my colors."

"Yeah, Nacho, you are. You are. You crazy. Someday, you'll go off to prison, you know that? "

"Yep, someday. I don't care. They can stick me in the 'lectric chair, and I'm goin' to stare them in the eyes and let them know I hate them and I am proud," Nacho said stoically as he put his pistol back in the front of his pants.

Jaime reached into his shirt pocket, pulled out a joint, and lit up. "Crazy. You are crazy. Good to have you on my side. Here, let's chill a bit. I need it; you need it, too." He handed the joint to Nacho, and as he did nacho noticed Jaime's hand was shaking.

As Nacho put the joint to his lips, the musty, sweet, skunky aroma filled his nose. "Where'd you get this? I think this is some of the worst I've had."

Jaime laughed. "My little bro, he got this at school. Carlos brought it home and was afraid my mom was gonna find it and take it for herself. So, he hid it under my pillow. Stupid, huh? I have a cold, right? So, there I am lying in bed and I feel somethin under my pillow. He comes walkin into the room and sees me with it. Carlos starts trying to fight me for it. I slapped him down hard, man."

By the time they got to Jaime's house, there were several cars there. Frankie's friends were there drinking beer. Tony, like always, was there. As they walked in the front door, one of Frankie's friends handed Nacho a beer.

"I saw you chasing those Voto's. You did good, man."

"Nacho is hangin' with us tonight, Frankie." Tony patted Nacho on the back, "Good to have you with us." After a few beers and talk, Tony walked into the bathroom.

"Nacho, were'd you get that piece? That is some fine lookin' piece," asked Frankie. Nacho looked down and realized his pistol was showing out from under his tee shirt.

"Where you think? I took it from a Vato. I was walkin' out from behind the store by the gas station, and this little gansta' comes walkin up to me and tries to start somethin'. So, I busted him up pretty bad. He weren't nothin'. He was lying there on the ground crying and bloody. So, to help him along, I shoved my heel into his face. Broke a few of his teeth, too. He had this Taurus on him. I took it."

"We may need that tonight, Nacho," whispered Frankie. "What'cha whispering about?," asked Jaime. "Nothin' concerning you. You just stay out of the way. You already gots one eye missing, you get hit in your good one and you're just wastin' space." Nacho looked at Jaime and laughed, "Yeah, you just keep an eye out for anything." Tony came walking out of the bathroom laughing. "Good one, Nacho! Yeah, Jaime, 'keep an eye out'." Jaime smiled and turned away to go to the bathroom. "Better take careful aim!," yelled Frankie. The laughter increased.

As the group made their way to one of the cars, Frankie asked Nacho to sit in the front passenger seat, "Just in case anything happens." As they were driving, they came to a stop light. Another car pulled up next to them. It was a patrol car. The officer looked over at the group for a passing moment, then looked over at his screen. When the light turned green, Frankie held back and let the patrol car go ahead. The patrol car slowed down, and Frankie decided it was best to take a detour. They turned into a residential area and saw a white couple walking their dogs.

"Dogs probably eat better than we do,"

quipped Jaime. No one responded.

Once Frankie felt it was okay, they turned around and went back on the main road and turned on Cooley Drive and parked in front of a house.

"Nacho, I want you to stand outside the car and wait for me," said Frankie as he grabbed a bag of weed and walked to the door of the house.
Nacho got out of the car, and realized that this was the life he wanted. Frankie was depending on him. He was respecting him. As Nacho stood there with his chin up and arms crossed, he felt like he was in charge.
He was a soldier of the street.

Frankie returned to the car and as they got in, Frankie had a smile on his face. "Let's party!," he said. As they drove away, Nacho turned the radio up.
 The next morning, Nacho realized he had so much beer and weed that he had passed out. He was sleeping it off on a couch, but he didn't recognize where he was. He made his way to the bathroom, and then went outside. He

figured he was about two blocks from home, so he slowly walked along the street. Something seemed different. He couldn't quite place it, but something seemed different. Was it the hangover? His mouth had the taste of stale smoke and beer. As he reached to pull up his pants, he realized his pistol was gone. One of Frankie's friends had taken it. As Nacho walked up to the door of his house, his mother came walking out of her bedroom.

"Mico, where have you been? You stink. Have you been drinking and smoking? Mico, my Mico!" His mother began to cry and turned away. Just at that moment, Marcello walked into the room.

"You becomin' a man? Huh? You gots a ways to go. You ain't even drivin' yet. You're only eleven. You ain't nothin'."

As the weeks passed, Nacho began to realize his life wasn't at home. What home was it? It wasn't a home like on T.V. His friends understood. They respected him.

VI

A trip

"Wake up, Mico. C'mon, wake up. Its time for church, remember?"

It was his mother, and she seemed a bit hurried.

"Mico, what time did you go to bed last night? I told you we were going to church. Hurry up, get ready."

"Church? Oh, yeah. How much time do I have?"

"Not much, I told you to get up almost twenty minutes ago, don't you remember? You didn't wake up, did you? Hurry up!"

Looking around his small room, he didn't see anything to wear that didn't have some dirt of wrinkles. Still, he knew he'd have to find something. It would be good to be out of the house, anyway. Marcello was sleeping off his night before, and Mico knew he had to be quiet; otherwise, the house would be in an uproar.

As he quickly dressed, he remembered the girl he met at church. "Mary, that was her name.

She was cute. I hope she's there," he thought to himself. He didn't feel like eating anything for breakfast, but that was probably just as good. The less he made noise, the better. Mico's mother was standing by the door waiting for him. She had put on some perfume, and the clean, delicate scent seemed out of place in the house with Marcello's stink in the air.

"Don't you want to grab something to eat before we leave?"

"No, that's okay mom. I'm ready and it really doesn't matter if I eat."

Once at church, Mico had wished he'd eaten something. His stomach began to growl and gurgle. His mother glanced over at him with a smile.

"We'll get something to eat after church if they don't have something here."

Mico's attention quickly turned to an announcement being made. There was going to be a trip to Disneyland for the church kids who could go.

"Disneyland? WHOA!," thought Mico. He'd seen the commercials on the television, and heard kids at school talking about it. There were rides and food. It sounded like fun, but suddenly he remembered home. There was no way he could go, not with the family situation and all. It would cost, and how would he get there?

Right about that time, the pastor's daughter, Vangie, came over to him. Very excited, she said, "Mijo, Felix and I are going to take you, Mary, Daniel, and Angie to Disneyland." Nacho was excited because he had always wanted to go there, but at the same time he didn't know if he should believe her. He'd heard promises like that before, and they were usually broken." Stuff like that doesn't happen to me," he thought to himself. Throughout the week, the thought of Disneyland filled his thoughts. He didn't see much of his friends that week, but Jaime came around twice to visit.

When Saturday came, Nacho couldn't believe that he was actually going to Disneyland. He walked to the church early that morning and waited for the cars to show up.

Time seemed to drag, and doubt plauged him. "Am I really going to go to Disneyland, or is this some kinda joke?" Suddenly, a car pulled into the parking area at the church. It was Felix and Vangie. The car was already filled with other kids, but there was room for him. As he got into the car, Mary smiled. "Hi, Nacho! Good to see you here." Daniel, a boy a around Nacho's age looked over and nodded in approval.

The drive to Disneyland was something Nacho had never experienced. Mary and Daniel started singing, and the others joined in. Vangie and Felix talked about God, and how life is a blessing to be enjoyed. Nacho started to feel like a kid again. He started to think to himself how much he would love to have mouse ears like he saw the kids wearing on T.V. When they fiinally arrived in the parking lot, Nacho could hardly believe it. There he was at Disneyland! The parking lot was almost full, and the walk to the gate seemed endless. "It seems a bit smaller than I thought it would," he thought to himself.

Nacho's uncle was there with the church group. His uncle, Nacho's mom's brother, was very involved at the church. Every time he saw him, it seemed like his uncle was trying to stay distant.

His uncle walked over to Nacho and whispered, " Remember, I am holding your money for you. I want to make sure you don't waste it."

"Waste it?" Nacho thought to himself. "Waste it on what? Drugs? You think that is all I'm about?"

"Yeah, okay. Uncle, where are you gonna be so I can find you?"

"I'm not just here to watch over you, Nacho. I'm here for some fun. So, you'll just need to look for me."

"Well, can I have some of the money now?"

Vangie and Felix came walking over. "C'mon, we want to get in there. The lines aren't getting any shorter, you know." Felix stared at Nacho's uncle for a moment. "What's up?"

"Oh, nothing. Nacho needs some of his

cash, that's all. Here ya go." His uncle acted like the money was coming out of his pocket, but Nacho knew his mother had given the money to him. As he gave the money to Nacho, he gave him a cold stare. "And what do you say?"

"Thank you, his uncle." As he spoke, he glanced at Felix. Felix had a look of disgust, and Nacho knew it was because of the way his uncle was acting.

Vangie was excited about Disneyland; her exuberance was infectious.

"C'mon! Why are you guys just standing here? Let's GO!"

The crowds of people pushed and shoved, but it didn't bother Nacho. He was at Disneyland, and nothing could go wrong.

While standing in lines isn't fun for most people, it gave Nacho an opportunity to talk to Mary and Daniel. After one ride, he ate a small breakfast at a stand because he wanted to save money for the mouse ears. As he started looking for his uncle, he saw one of the stands that sold the mouse ears. A bunch of kids and their parents were there, and Goofy was walking around having pictures taken with them.

Everything seemed surreal, and everyone seemed to be acting younger than their age. Parents and kids were laughing.

"Pretty cool, huh?" It was Mary, and she had a bag of candy. "Want some? Its pretty good."

"Okay, thanks. Which candy is this?"

"Some kind of toffee. I don't like the green ones, though. They taste kinda wierd."

Nacho looked in the bag and took a green toffee.

"You don't need to do that, Nacho. I just said I didn't like them. You could take a different color if you want."

"Nah, that's okay. I'll take a green one and see how bad they really taste."

Both of them started to laugh, and Nacho noticed Mary had a sparkle in her eyes. She was pretty.

"I'm looking for my uncle to get some more money for the mouse ears. Have you seen him around at all?"

"Um, yeah. I think I saw him over there," she said pointing over to a large tree. "I think he was talking to Vangie."

"Great! I'll be back in a sec."

As he went in the direction of the tree, Nacho saw his uncle sipping on a soda.

'Hey!"

"Hey, Nacho. What's up?"

"Could I have some more of my money? I want to buy some mouse ears."

"You used your money, Nacho. There isn't any more left for you."

"What? You didn't give me all the money. I hardly used anything. I took one ride and ate some breakfast. I was saving the money for some mouse ears."
"Nacho, you used it up. I told you. Now don't go getting an attitude with me." Nacho glared at his uncle, but could feel tears welling up.

"How? How did I use all the money?"
"Nacho, you used it. That's final, okay? Now quit makin' a scene. Grow up, would you?"

Pretty much the day was over, and

Nacho walked back to the car by himself. Mary saw him leaving the park, and followed him through the crowd back to the car.

"Nacho, what's going on? Why are you upset? Why are you leaving?"
He told her about his uncle and the money, and how he just wanted some mouse ears. As they spoke, he sensed Mary's compassion. She tried to comfort him. Suddenly, Angie, Daniel, and Felix came to the car. At that point, he felt sick to his stomach. Sitting in the car without shade, the car became hot. His anger fueled his feelings. His uncle had lied, and was ruining a perfectly good trip. He knew there was still some money left. Disneyland wasn't that fun after all. About an hour passed, and Vangie came walking over.

"What's going on? Nacho, are you alright?" Vangie's voice was warm and kind.

"Its his uncle," said Felix, "He told Nacho there wasn't any more money left. "

Vangie shook her head. "Nacho, its going to be okay. We should be going anyway. Why don't you come and sit by the door in case you feel like throwing up. Okay? We'll have the window open for you so you can get some fresh air. That will make you feel better."

On the way back home, Nacho was depressed because his whole day was ruined. He stared out the window and looked at the cars on the freeway. He closed his eyes and went to sleep.

Suddenly, he woke up.   He couldn't believe what he was seeing. The car was upside down and bodies were everywhere. People were running around screaming, and the cops were opening the door with the Jaws of Life. When they were pulling Nacho out, he kept saying, "I need my jacket because my mom is going to be mad at me." He didn't know what the ambulance guy meant when he said, "Believe me son, she won't be mad." That was the last thing Nacho heard before everything went black. He passed out.

"Doctor Johnson to ICU. Doctor Johnson to ICU." The announcement awoke Nacho and he looked around for someone. He was alone in a hospital room. It was quiet. He tried to sit up, but his side hurt. He moved his legs, and then his arms. His head throbbed. He checked the room, and saw a television set on the wall. There were all sorts of machines near him, but nothing was hooked up to him.

"Hey! Hey!" The more he shouted, the more his side hurt.

Just then, a nurse walked in.

"Do you need something for the pain?"

"Uh, no. Where is everybody? What happened? Why am I in here? Where's my mom? What's going on?

"You need to relax, okay? Just try and relax. I know it hurts." The nurse had a paper in her hand, and was reading it. "I want to ask you some questions, okay?"

"Yeah, okay."

"What is your name?

"Ignacio. Ignacio Pizano. What's going on?"

"Just relax, Ignacio. Can you tell me how old you are?"

"Eleven. I'm eleven."

"Good. When is your birthday, Ignacio?"

" October. Its October 14, 1964. Hey, c'mon. What's going on? Where are Vangie and Felix? Where are Mary and Daniel? Why don't you answer me?"

The nurse looked at him for a moment. "Your doctor will be in shortly. Your mom is coming to see you later. Right now, I am going to give you something to help you relax."

Just then, Nacho realized he had a needle stuck in his arm attached to a bag hanging from a pole. The nurse took out a syringe from her pocket and put the needle in a Y-shaped area in the tube.

"I don't need no….," suddenly, he felt warm and relaxed; he was sleepy, in fact.

When he awoke again, he was wondering where my mom was. He could hear the sounds of the hospital. People were talking quietly outside his room, and occasionally he would hear the nurse call-alarm from another patient. There were sounds of televisions echoing in the hall. It wasn't long before his uncle Paul showed up, which was a little weird for him because he had not seen him in years.

Paul sat down in a chair next to the bed and said, "I have something serious to tell you. Vangie, Felix, Mary, and Daniel were dead. Angie is at another hospital in critical condition, Nacho.   She is in pretty bad shape, I'm afraid. It is most likely she's not going to make it."

"What? What the...what happened? We were coming home from Disneyland. What happened?" Nacho started crying. The tears showered down his face. "Mary? Mary is gone? They're all gone? Vangie and Felix are gone? How? Why? What am I...," the words came out of his mouth between the gasps for breath as he cried.

"I'm sorry, Nacho. I truly am. It was an accident. I guess Felix must've fallen asleep at the wheel. The car rolled down the embankment. Do you remember anything?" Paul's words sounded warm and sincere.

"No. No, I don't I just can't believe it. This isn't really happening. We were just coming back from Disneyland. I wasn't feeling good and I fell asleep. Why did this happen? Why?" Nacho started crying so hard he could hardly catch his breath. Paul stepped out of the room for a moment, and nurse came in carrying another syringe. She put the needle in the Y-shaped thing, and Nacho started to feel relaxed. He cried until he fell asleep.

The next day, the discharge nurse came in with Nacho's mother.

"Mico! Mi Corazón! I love you so much." His mother's tears and hugs made him feel better. "Mico, you are alive. I know what happened, and I am so sorry. Felix and Vangie were good friends, and everybody has been talking about the accident. We're flying home. The nurse is here to get your things. I have your medications. Oh, mi corazón, I love you." His mother kept talking to him, but things were not right. As he was wheeled down the hall to the door of the hospital, it all seemed like a bad nightmare. Nacho said little, but guilt started to beat his spirit. He was confused, and didn't know whether to cry, be angry, or be happy because he made it.

When they finally arrived home, his mom told him she felt that God had a plan for his life. "That is why He saved you, Mico. God is all powerful and loving. He knows you, Mico. He loves you. You survived because he has a plan for you, you'll see."

"Mom, I kinda feel weird, because I don't even remember what happened. I feel like...I dunno...I guess, I..." A knock on the door interrupted him; it was the older home boys from the neighborhood.

"Please mijo, don't go with them. Just see what they want, but don't go with them. This is your time to turn your life to God, Mico. Please."

"I gotta answer the door, mom. I'll see what they want."

Somehow, the older boys heard about the accident and came to see if Nacho was okay. They gave him a bag of weed. It might have not been the right present, but they showed that they cared by giving him a present. He looked to see if his mom saw what happened, but she had left the room. He stuffed it in his pants.

Tony looked at him and said, "Man,

Nacho that was close. So, like, how you doin'? You feelin' alright?"

"Yeah, kinda. I'm hurtin' a bit, but I'm okay."

"Sorry to hear about your friends, dude. That sucks."

"Yeah. Hey, I gotta go and rest. Thanks for the weed."

For the next few days, Nacho thought about the accident and rested. He still found it hard to believe he was alive, and the others died. He asked his mom if she had heard about how Angie was, but she said she hadn't heard anything. She thought Angie had probably died in the hospital."

"Mico, tomorrow we're going to go to church and thank God for saving you. I know God loves you, Mico. He has big plans for you. It wasn't your time to go. You have important things to do here. Everyone has a part of God's plan, and I think he wants you to do something great."

That Sunday, Nacho and his mom went to church.

"Mom, I don't know what to expect. I mean, I survived the accident and the others didn't. What is going to happen?"

"We're going to church to worship God and thank him. I know you feel bad about the accident, Mico, but things are as they are. You survived, and that is all that matters. You aren't responsible for what happened. God isn't responsible for what happened. He wants only good things for us. There are things in life we have control over, and things we don't. God turns even the bad things that happen toward what he wants."

Nacho listened to her words, and believed them.

When they got to church, Nacho saw people were gathered together in small groups. Some were talking; others were listening and shaking their heads. Some were crying; others had their hands on others' shoulders.

When some of the people saw Nacho, he was given dirty looks. When he walked by one group of people, they turned away as if he wasn't there. A woman, walked over to Nacho.

He smiled at her as she approached. "You should have been the one to die, not Vangie the pastor's daughter." Another woman agreed. "Vangie had so much to give, but you? Look at you! Mary was so sweet, but you?" They had no love, no compassion, and no sympathy for Nacho at all. He could not help but to think to himself that the gangsters from his neighborhood showed that they cared for him more than the people in the church did. At least they came by and gave him some weed.

When he saw his uncle, he walked over to him. As he passed a couple of people, they stared at him like he was an insect.

," I...I...I need to tell you something. People are saying stuff like I shoulda died. I can't understand. Why..."

His uncle interrupted him, "Because of who your father is, and most likely you are gonna be just like him. They are probably right." Nacho's uncle turned, and walked away; Nacho was alone.

As far as he was concerned, that day

God and church had lost him forever.

VII

Nobody

Weeks became months, and Nacho had decided being with his friends was where he belonged. His mom nagged him about going to church with her, but he made up his mind that the church held nothing for him. God didn't want him, either. "Nice thoughts, mom, but reality is where it is," he thought to himself. The accident became a distant memory, but Mary haunted his thoughts. He thought about her often, and wondered what could have been had she lived. She was the only one who took the time to see him for who he really was deep down inside. He reminded himself, though, that she was gone. She died. There wasn't any way of bringing her back, and it was a waste of time to think about something that just wasn't going to be. Partying with his friends became a way of doing life, and school was nothing.

Frankie was coming over to the house at 2:30 that afternoon. The fog was coming in, and it seemed to be a colder day than usual.

"Mom? Mom!"

"You hear what the weather is supposed to be?"

"Mico, since when do you ever pay attention to the weather? It's Saturday. You got something so important that the weather is going to bother you?"

"No. I'm hangin' with my friends this afternoon, that's all."

"Mico, I wish you wouldn't. Why can't you stay here for a bit?"

"He's got things to do? Huh?" Marcello chimed into the conversation. "You got something to do? You can do something for me. Hand me that." Marcello was lying on the couch smoking a cigarette. He grabbed the top of the couch with one hand, lifted himself up, and pointed over to crumpled up bag. "Gimme that. Right there. Gimme that."

As he grabbed the bag, Nacho tossed it to Marcello. "Here."

"Here? Here? Like, go fetch kinda 'here'? Don't talk to me like that! I tell you to do somethin', and you do it. You understand?

Here. Here. Like I'm some kinda dog or somethin'. Nacho, don't you talk to me like that!" Marcello's voice was getting louder and his face was red. Nacho knew he should leave. Marcello had a way of getting himself worked up, especially when he had been drinking.

Slamming the door as he walked out, he made his way down the street to Frankie's. Walking down the street, he tied on his bandana. When he got there, Jaime opened the door and Nacho walked in. He could smell something cooking, and thought maybe there would be something there for him to eat.

"Hey, whatch'a doin'?" asked Jaime

"I thought I'd come over instead of Frankie comin' over to pick me up. How's things?"

"Fine, but I heard you and Frankie and Tony were going out tonight. Mind if I come along?"

"No, but you better check with Frankie. I think we've got some business first. Then, we're goin' to hang out over at some guy's house. So, what is that you got cooking?"

"Oh, yeah…want some? I made some canned spaghetti and threw in a can of tomatoes. Mom gets them at the cannery just like yours does, only she's got a deal with one of the managers there. So, we get more cans than we need."

"Sure, you got some? I'll eat. Got some beer?"

"Beer? Yeah, mom picked up a case yesterday. We got some."

As Nacho and Jaime sat in front of the TV, Carlos walked in from his bedroom. He grabbed Jaime's beer and took a few gulps.

"How old are you, Carlos?" Nacho asked.

"Old enough. Why? You got a problem with me drinking beer?"

Nacho laughed, "Heck, no. Why don't you grab me another." Two beers later, Frankie drove up. Jaime and Nacho walked outside to greet him.

"Frankie, Nacho said yous guys are going for a ride then going to party. Mind if I come along?" Frankie ignored him, and looked at Nacho.

"What are you doin' here? I thought I was gonna pick you up?"

"Marcello."

"He still beatin on you and your mom? When's he gonna leave?"

"Soon, I hope."

"You stick close to us, homes. He ain't nothin' but wasted all the time. Nacho, you're better stayin' away from him. You're one of us."

"Yep, I am. You alls my family. You alls the family I need."

"You guys been startin' the party early. I can smell the beer on you. You wasted, Nacho?"

"No, not yet...but I plan to be."

Jaime got into Frankie's car.

"Bro, you better be ready to squeeze in here cuz me, Nacho, and Tony are goin' to Enrique's house. We gonna pick him up, get some gas, and then we got some business to take care of. Then, we're goin' over to some guy's house to party."

Jaime looked at Nacho and said, "Sounds cool to me, esse!"

They spun the car around and Tony was sitting outside on his porch. He was flying his colors big time-shirt and bandana were the same color.

They got to the corner of Biscayne and South King Road, and Jaime threw up outside the car.

"Dude! Man, I tell you. I can't take you no place and yous acting like a swata. Get out and walk home!" Nacho started laughing.

"Is your brother for real?" Tony asked. Frankie ignored the remark. Tony looked at Frankie, and asked, "So, we gonna get Enrique? Dude is insane. Not as insane as you, Nacho, but crazy."

Nacho felt good hearing that. Crazy. Yeah, crazy. They picked up Ricky, and drove to a park. Sitting in the car for about ten minutes, they waited. The smell of a barbecue wafted through the air. Nacho scoped out the park and saw a family sitting on the grass having a picnic. A Ford Pinto drove by slowly on the other side of the park, and then stopped.

"Let's go," Tony said. The four of them got out of the car and started walking over to the Pinto. Four Enemies got out, flying their colors and cussing. Walking across the park, Nacho saw the family suddenly start picking up their belongings and grabbing the children. Nacho could feel his body tense up. His heart started pounding, and the fight began. From the corner of his eye, he saw Frankie take on a guy who weighed in at about 200 pounds. He couldn't see Ricky or Tony, only a man about twenty-five coming for him. The man outweighed Nacho, but that didn't matter. Nacho charged at the man, kept his balance, and started beating the man's face with his fists. He could smell the man's sweat and blood, or was that his own? It didn't matter; he was going to beat the man down…down to the ground, down into the dirt. Nacho felt a blow to his left cheek, but the hit slid down to his shoulder. He didn't feel the pain, just the rage.

The anger that was pent up inside came out roaring, and he was pounding away his rage. As the man fell to his knees, Nacho started kicking with his foot at an angle. He slammed the man's face once, twice, and then a swift kick to the side of his head. The side kick threw Nacho off balance for a moment. It was then that he realized the man was unconscious. Blood was smeared across the man's nose and jaw. His ear was bleeding, and blood was splattered across the man's white tee shirt.

Nacho spun around and saw Tony and Frankie were holding their ground, but Ricky was getting beaten pretty badly. The guy suddenly pulled out a knife and started swinging it at Ricky, who jumped back each time the blade cut the air. Nacho ran towards the man.

"Nacho, don't. Wait, man," yelled Ricky. The man quickly turned to see who Ricky was yelling to. When he did, Ricky jumped him. Nacho grabbed the hand holding the knife and began twisting it. He wanted to twist the man's hand off. He heard a dull snap, and the knife dropped to the ground. Nacho held on, but the man struggled to get away. Before he knew it, the man was running over to the man Nacho had beaten earlier. That guy was getting up, and the two of them were limping back to the Pinto. The guy Tony was fighting suddenly pulled out a pistol and started waving it at Tony. Tony backed off, but Frankie pulled out a pistol. Nacho recognized it; it was his pistol. As the two holding pistols yelled at each other, the other Enemies started backing away. They got into the Pinto and drove off.

"We got 'em! Rifamos" Tony yelled.

"Yeah, they're not going to be here for awhile. C'mon, let's go over an party!"

When they were in the car, Tony looked at Nacho.

"You are crazy! You're so crazy, man! I couldn't believe that. Did you see what he did to that guy's face? It was like…man…you are a true blood, man. True! That guy running from us… what a pendejo!"

Nacho sat there without expression. He

didn't say a word for a few minutes as the others were bragging about the fight. Finally, he spoke.

"Frankie, I want my pistol, my fusca. I want it back, now."

As he was driving, he turned to the back seat to look at Nacho.

"Sure, sure. I found it, you know. Man, I found it sitting there at my house. You were so wasted, man, I think you dropped it or something. Yeah, you dropped it, esse". As Frankie said this, Tony, who was sitting in the front seat, had a big smile on his face. "Yeah," Tony repeated, "Yeah, man, I think you dropped it or something." Frankie and Tony chuckled, but Nacho didn't find it amusing.

"I sure hope yous ain't laughing at me. If you are, I'll take the both of yous on right now. Give me my pistol back, Frankie."

Frankie reached down onto the front seat and gave the pistol to Nacho, and said, "Like we've been saying. You are a true soldier."

When they arrived at the party, there

were several girls there along with some of the older guys Nacho recognized.

There was one man there who seemed to be respected. Everyone gave him respect, and he was in charge.

"Hey, jefe, we took care of those Vato's out by the park. They ain't gona be around. You shoulda seen ol' Nacho, he's a warrior. He took on this one guy and beat him down good. I think he busted the guy's jaw or something," Tony said excitedly.

The man took a look at Nacho. "You Marcello's son?"

"Yeah," Nacho answered.

"Good job, Nacho," the man said. Nacho thought for a moment. This man knew his name? He knew Marcello?

"Nacho, were running low on beer. Go get some, would you? Tony, take Nacho down to the store and get some. We got a party going on."

"You got it," Nacho answered quickly. "Whoa, this man is asking me to go and do something for him? He respects me!" Nacho thought to himself.

As he drove Nacho to the store, he said, "Nacho, this is big time. This man is in for life. For life, you understand me? If he is looking at you-respecting you, man…you are in." Nacho felt fine with the thought that he was 'in'. When they got to the store, Nacho stood tall, proud, and walked in. The clerk was an older man who seemed nervous. Nacho liked that. He knew he intimidated the old man, and that was good. It felt good to have people afraid of him. That meant the old man respected him. He grabbed couple of cases of Schaefer beer, and went to the counter. "That is three dollars per twelve pack, so that will be six dollars plus tax." The man didn't bother to ask Nacho for his ID. Nacho knew he was afraid. He paid the man, and walked back to the car. He felt like a man. He was feared; he was respected.

Tony laughed when Nacho got in the car. "Man, you got that Vato's blood all over your shirt. Did you know that, man? You got your pistol on, too. See that, esse? You see that bulge stickin' out under your tee shirt?"

Nacho looked down at his shirt. Sure enough, there was blood splattered all over his shirt. Sure enough, he was wearing his pistol. He was still wearing his bandana, too. "No wonder the clerk was nervous," he chuckled to himself.

The party went late, and there was plenty of weed and beer. The girls were getting wasted, and the guys laughing about it. A few of the guys went into the kitchen and started pulling out all sorts of food. Nacho ate a can of Hershey's chocolate syrup and chips, cookies, and whatever else was there. It was well past midnight when Tony told him he'd take him home.

"First, we gonna drop by that park. Esse, I gots a can of spray paint in the trunk. When we get there, let's tag."

When they pulled up to the park, it was dark. Off in the distance, they saw a public restroom. Quickly, they ran over to the cinderblock wall. Nacho took the can and painted

4 EVER

4 LIFE GANGA

They ran back to the car, and drove to Nacho's house. His head was spinning. What a day!

When he came through the front door, he saw Marcello lying on the couch. He was passed out, and there was a syringe sitting on the table next to him. He must have been shooting up. A couple of beer cans were scattered on the floor around him, and the TV was on. Nacho stood still and looked at him. "What if I wasted him right now? What if I did him right now, and wiped the pistol off and stuck it in his hand? People might think he'd done himself. Mom and me, we'd be free of all of this." Nacho slowly took out his pistol, and released the safety. Quietly, he stepped over to Marcello and put the gun at the side of his head. Marcello's eyes opened up and stared at Nacho.

"I could do this right now. Right now, you hear me? Don't you never touch my mom or me again. You understand? Never." His voice was quiet, but firm.

"Do it. Do it, kid. Do it. You don't have the guts, do you?" Marcello sneered.

Nacho lowered the gun and clicked on the safety.

"You ain't nobody. Nobody. You ain't no son of mine. If you was, you'd have done it. You…," Marcello passed out again.
As Nacho turned to walk away, he thought he heard Marcello's raspy chuckle. "Nobody, you ain't nobody. Never was. Never will be."

The next day, Marcello moved out of the house.

VIII

Cross and Double-Crossed

The months that followed, Nacho became closer to his friends. They seemed to understand him. He was going in deeper into the Homeboys, and some felt he would be a good soldier of the streets. He, too, felt that his life was taking him that way. Fight after fight, drug deal after drug deal, Nacho was becoming a respected member even though he was only thirteen. The older guys in the hood respected him, and he them.

"Mico, you hafta go to school today. I got a call from the school, and they said you weren't there last week. I can't keep writing excuse notes for you. They'll come over here and take you if you don't attend. Do you hear me?" His mother was angry, but he figured she'd get over it if he went to school for a few days.

"Yeah, mom, I'm going...I'm going. What is there at that stupid school for me anyways? The teachers don't like me, and I don't like them. I don't know hat they're doing half the time. I just sit in class…its like being in prison."

"Being in prison? Being in prison? What the…? I…I don't know what to do with you. You were so good and now you're like you don't care anymore. I am getting sick of this, do you hear me? Sick! Look at what you've become. Is this what you want for your life? Is this what God saved you for? You think that?"

Just at that moment, Nacho's older sister Marcella, walked into the room. Unlike Rachel, his other sister who wasn't around much, Marcella had moved back into the house when Marcello left.

"What is all the noise? I can't even sleep with all this yelling going on. Mom, why are you so upset?," Marcella asked.

"Why do you think? Look at your brother. We might as well have your father here for the way Nacho is acting."

Marcella glared at Nacho and said, "She has a good point. Look at you. You're acting like your some big shot 'gangsta'…hanging around in the hood with your 'homes', wearing that stupid bandana you got on your head. You keep doing that, and we're going to be going to your funeral. You dress like that; you act like that, and somebody's going to take a shot at you just because."

'Marcella, you and mom don't know me at all. You don't, do you? I AM a homeboys, in my blood. It's me. I am, and I get more respect out there than I do here, or at school, or at that church you go to. Nobody knows me or cares for me except for them. I can be who I am, and I ain't judged."

"Ain't judged?" His mom interrupted. "You ain't judged? Look at you. You don't think people out there are judging you all the time by the way you act and dress? Quit being what they want, and be who you are. Find out who you are without them telling you who to be."

"What? You don't think people at school and church aren't telling me who to be, too? You even tellin' me who I'm supposed to be.

Everybody tellin' everybody else who they supposed to be." Nacho's anger was rising, and he knew he'd start cussing like his dad if his mom and sister didn't get off his back.

"I'm outta here. Later."

Marcella stood next to her mother, who was crying. Marcella mocked Nacho…"Outta here. Latter. Bye mister big gansta dude! Bye big man."

As Nacho slammed the door and walked down the driveway, the door opened.

Marcella was standing in the doorway. She yelled, "Hey mister gansta, hey mr. gansta! You forgot your school book, mister gansta. Look everybody, it's a gansta." She threw his books across the walkway at him. Nacho turned and picked up the books, and walked away. The neighbor across the street, an old man, looked over at the commotion.

"What you lookin' at, ol' man? You got a problem or somethin'?"

The old man looked away and shook his head, mumbling something.

"What? What, ruco? What?"

The old man limply waved his
weathered hand at Nacho, and walked back
into his home.

As he walked to school, his anger was fuming.
"What am I doing here?," he thought to himself,
"This is so stupid. I could be hangin' out havin'
a beer and a joint with my friends. Yeah,
kickin' it and havin' a good time. Instead, here I
am goin' to some stupid school." As he was
walking up to the school he saw Carlos, the kid
with the bad breath.

"Hey, Nacho! Long time. How's it
goin'?"

"I'm here, ain't I. I could be hanging with
my boys, but here I am. So, what?"

"No, dude, I was just asking how you're
doing. That's all. I didn't mean anything by it.
You can't be flying colors at school. That's
against the rules, and the teachers will be all
over your case."

"So? They can't tell me what to wear.
I'm a Homeboy. I am with the La Ganga. I am
true."

"Nacho, please don't do that. You've

been a good friend when we've seen each other. My brother, he was shot cuz he belonged. That's why we moved here from Sunnyvale. Please, Nacho…"

"Dude, shaddup. You don't know nothin'. Man, if you was in a gang, you wouldn't need a pistol. Your breath would knock 'em out."

Carlos scowled, and had a hurt expression on his face. Angelina, a girl who had overheard the talking, walked up to Nacho- right in his face.

"You used to be so cool. Now, you're a jerk. You're a real jerk, you know that? Acting like some kinda fool. You don't think people are laughing behind your back at the stupid things you do?"

"Lucky you're a girl, Angelina. If you was a guy, I'd knock that face of yours clean off."

"Ooohhh, so, you into hittin' girls? Angelina started laughing loudly, and attracting attention. Some other kids started to gather around to see what was going on. As the crowd gathered, the yard duty supervisor walked over.

"I just said, if you was a guy I'd knock your face off. But, you're just a girl. You ain't nothin'. You ain't worth hittin'." With that, Nacho turned around and walked off the campus. He walked to Tony's house, and knocked on the door. Tony was slow in getting to the door, he must've been sleeping.

"Hey, I'm going to hang here for awhile, okay with you?"

"Uh, yeah...yeah. I, uh...I got some company, but you can hang here in the living room for awhile."

Nacho turned on the TV, kicked back on the couch. Covered with old, dirty blankets, Nacho decided to take a nap. He awoke, briefly, to see a girl leaving the house. "Must be one of Tony's girlfriends," he thought. He fell back asleep until Tony came out from the bathroom wearing a towel around his waist. His hair was wet, and Nacho noticed the tattoos across Tony's chest and back.

"Cool lookin' tats. I want one of those."

"You can't have one of these. I'm wearing them right now," Tony chuckled. "But, I can get you in touch with a guy who does tats for all the guys. So, you want somethin' to eat? I think we got some food in the fridge. Let me check."

"Tony, he's cool. I wanna be just like him. He has it going," Nacho thought to himself. There was something about all of the guys that he admired.

"Here you go. Ain't much. We got some beer, I found some cookies. Here's a piece of chicken from a couple nights ago. I think we're good."

"Yeah, thanks esse. You got anything on for tonight?"

"Yeah, I do. We gotta drop off some weed at the park. If you want, why don't you take some of that over there on the table when you're done, and see if there's anyone interested over at the store parking lot. There are always a few people hangin' around, waitin'.

"Sounds fine, Tony. What time should I

be back?"

"Around seven. We'll leave from here. We'll take my car and head over for a party tonight."

Nacho finished his snack, looked at the wire-rimed clock on the kitchen wall, and figured he'd have about four hours to sell some weed. He took the bag and walked the two blocks over to the store. He found a spot behind the store in an alley, and waited. Sure enough, a car came driving by slowly with a couple of high school aged boys and a girl in the car. They were nicely dressed, and he thought they must have a lot of money.

The driver of the car lowered his window a bit and spoke in a normal tone to Nacho.

"Yo, kid. You know where I could get something?"

"First, I ain't no 'kid', and second, what it is you're lookin' for?" He heard someone laugh in the car.

"Weed. You know where I could get some weed?"

"Yeah, I do. You're interested?"

"Duh. Yeah! C'mon, let's see it."

Nacho showed them what he had.

"I got an ounce right here."

"How much?

"Forty bucks."

"Forty? Cool. We'll take it"

One of the guys in the car asked to check if first, so Nacho opened the bag for them to look. "It looks clean. Nice…real nice." As the driver reached into his pocket, he took out a roll of twenty dollar bills. He reeled of two, and gave them to Nacho.

"Where you from? You don't look local," Nacho asked.

"Saratoga."

"Out of your league, sport," one guy said in the back seat with the girl.

The girl frowned. "Hey," she said," Mike, you can be so stupid sometimes. Be polite. The guy is out here trying to do business. Besides, he's kinda cute."

"Nobody sells it there?," Nacho asked.

"Oh yeah, they grow it up around Canyon View Drive… in the hills, and over in

Los Gatos, but they charge too much for it. It isn't quality like this. Cindy, here, sells it at the theater. I can sell some over at the high school. My little brother can sell it over at the junior high. Why?"

"If you like the price, we can hook up. I can get you all you need."

"Sounds cool to me. If this is as good, I'll meet you here next week at the same time," the driver said.

"Yeah, I'll be here."

As the car drove off, Nacho looked at the money. He had sold more than Tony probably thought he would. Tony would be proud. Nacho started the short walk back to Tony's house. Wearing his bandana, he was showing his colors. He noticed people who drove by would look at him, so he picked his chin up a bit and had a serious look like he was bad…and he was.

Tony saw him walking up the driveway, and opened the door.

"Why are you back already?"

"Sold it. Sold the ounce. Here's the

money."

"Dang, man, you're a salesman. Good going! I think the party will start early, don't you? C'mon, let's get some beer and food. We're meeting over at a guy's house a few miles away. We better get going. Dang, we're two hours early. Cool!"

The stop at the store was brief, and by the time they got to the house there was a lot of cars already there. Tony parked his car around the corner about a block and a half away. The music was going, and people were walking in and out of the house. The air was filled with the mixture of pot and a barbecue. As they walked through the side gate, he could see hot dogs were grilling, and a chest of beer on ice was sitting under the patio roof. People were everywhere, and the party seemed to be a big one. The eating, drinking, and smoking was going on for a few hours. Some people left; others came. Soon, the beer and food were gone. Nacho, Tony, and some others decided to go since the party was going dry. As they started to walk over to the car, a young man came walking up. They figured he was heading to the party late.

"You all out of drink?"

Tony answered, "Yeah. Gone. You missed a party, man. It was good."

The man started laughing. "Well, come on over to my place. I got drink, food, and a movie."

Tony, Nacho, and the guys looked at each other. "Yeah, okay…sounds good," Tony said. They followed the man down the street and went through a side gate. There, on a table, was Kool-Aid, popcorn, chips, and some chairs set up to watch a film on the side of his house. The guys looked at each other in amazement. "No beer?," one of them asked. "No beer," the man said. But I got a great movie here, so what do you have to lose? Plenty of Kool-Aid, and I can always make more popcorn. The guys grabbed some cups of Kool-aid, popcorn, and sat down in the chairs.

"This is weird, esse," Nacho whispered.

"Yeah, this is…uh…different," one of the

other guys said.

The man started the film. It was "The Cross and the Switchblade." A couple of the guys started to laugh, but the more they sat and watched the film the more they got into the story. Nacho watched it, and thought about his mom. He thought about what she had said about God and there being more to his life. The film made him think about things he hadn't thought about before. The scenes in the film seemed like the life he was living in so many ways. When the film was over, the man told them that God had a plan for them, just like they heard in the film. That God loves them, and doesn't want this for them. Tony laughed. "Hey, man, thanks for the drinks and food. The movie was good, too. You keep on preaching, okay?" The guys got up from the chairs and walked out of the man's yard, but Nacho held back for a moment. "Thanks, man. Thanks."

The man's expression was kind and warm, almost like Nacho's mom in some strange way. "I'll tell you something. God has a plan for you. God loves you as his own.

Don't ever forget that."

"Yeah, well…umm…thanks, man," Nacho responded.

"You comin'?" It was Tony. He was ready to go and didn't want to wait around any longer than he had to.

"Yeah, I'm comin'. I'll be there. I ain't your dog, man. Don't be talkin' to me like that!"

Nacho could hear the guys laughing and hooting in the front of the house.

"Come on, esse, or I'll slap you."

"OOooo…listen to him! Slap him down? Nacho slap you down, fool!"

Nacho looked at the man. His look of compassion hit Nacho's heart.

"I gotta go. Thanks again."

"You can go, son, but God always finds you. You're always welcome to come here. Okay?"

Nacho nodded, and walked out to the front of the house. Tony and the guys were sitting in the car.

"What were you doin', homes? You havin' a private prayer meetin'?"

"Whatever, dude. He is a good man."

Tony stared at Nacho, giving him that chin-up, hard look. "Remember who you are, esse. Remember who is always here for you."

"Yeah, I do."

"Who is you, Nacho? Who your friends be, esse?"

"You know who I am. True."

Nacho was quiet on the drive home, but the others were talking constantly. They were all hyped up, and didn't want the night to end.

Nacho slipped into his house quietly. He didn't want to wake up Marcella or his mom. The morning had been enough for him, and he figured they probably talked about him most of the day anyway. He went into his room, and closed the door. He fell onto his bed and into a deep sleep.

"Nacho?" It was his mother whispering through the door. "Nacho?"

"Yeah, mom. What?"

"The phone, its for you. It's your father. He wants to talk to you."

"Yeah? Well, I don't want to talk to him."

He looked at the clock radio, it said it was one o'clock in the afternoon. He'd been sleeping for hours.

"Nacho, please. Just get up and talk to your father on the phone. He's calling from Las Vegas. He said he want to talk with you a minute."

"Yeah, yeah. Okay."

Nacho got up dizzily. He could smell the weed on him from the night before. His mouth had a dry, bitter taste in it. As he opened his bedroom door, Marcella was sitting on the couch with her legs and arms crossed. She didn't even look up or speak to him. She sat there, staring straight ahead as if he wasn't even there.

Nacho picked up the phone.

"Yeah."

"Hey, Nacho. Its me, your dad."

"Yeah."

"Nacho, I know things haven't been good between us. I want to...I want to make things better for us. I want to be a real father for you. I'm sorry for the way I acted to you.

Nacho, I want to start fresh. Can we do that?"

"Yeah, whatever. Is that all?"

"No, Nacho. I want you to come here to Vegas with me. I want you to have a fresh start with me here. Can we do that?"

"Vegas? Dad, I dunno. I mean, really? Vegas? Things would be that different? I dunno. I think it is a good idea we just stay away from each other. You know what I mean?"

"Nacho, I haven't been a dad to you. I truly want a fresh start. I…I think we could be together and things would be better. It could work, Nacho. Please?"

Nacho thought for a moment. Things could be better if he moved away. He pondered the idea of life in Las Vegas. It would be different.

"Umm…okay, yeah. Okay, I'll go. How will I get there?"

Marcella coughed, and made a snorting sound. Nacho turned to look at her, but she was still in the same position.

"Well, Nacho, I sent money for you to

get a ticket. You'll fly here. We can do this, son. We can. Today is…what is today? Oh yeah, today is Tuesday. So, could you pack and be ready to fly by Thursday?"

"Yeah. Yeah, I'll pack and see you on Thursday. I'll let mom set up the flight for me. Then, we'll let you know when I'll arrive there."

"Sounds great, Nacho. Things will be different, son. Really, they will."

"Okay, yeah. Well, I'll see you then. Bye."

"Bye, son."

As he hung up the phone, he could hardly believe it. His father was having a change of heart toward him? As he turned to put the phone down, Marcella said, "So, you're going? Good. Maybe there will be some peace here. No more of your 'homes' hangin' around making life miserable. I'm sick of them."

His mother came walking in from the kitchen, and looked down at the floor. "Mico, I wish things were different. I really do. I can't handle you, Mico. I just can't anymore.

Marcello has said he can handle you better than I can."

"I love you mom. I do. I guess this is the best all around."

Marcella chimed in, "The best? Darn right it is. I can't see you going anywhere here. I am..."

Nacho's mom stopped Marcella abruptly, "Nacho is your brother. We discussed this yesterday, and I think we both came to some agreement. Didn't we, Marcella? Mico, I know this will be a change. I'll make the arrangements for you. I love you, Mico. I always have; I always will. You know that."

It was a change. Whew, what a change. Nacho thought about the move, and what it meant. What few things he had to pack, he did. They all fit into a small suitcase his mom had. He thought if he packed that afternoon, he could tell his friends goodbye tonight and tomorrow.

"Mom, I'm going out to say bye to the guys!" His mom was in her room, and her voice sounded distant. "Okay, Mico. Please, don't stay out late."

"Big surprise. Holmes is going out to be with his friends," Marcella said.

Nacho ignored the remark, and walked out. Bandana on, flannel shirt buttoned only on top over his tee shirt, he walked out. Walking down to Frankie and Jaime's house, he saw Carlos sitting on the porch wearing his bandana.

"Hey, esse. Where's your brothers?"

"Inside."

"What you doin' out here?"

"Maybe it isn't any of your business, man. I'm just chillin'."

Walking past Carlos, he walked into the house. Jaime was in his room; Frankie came in through the back door. "Hey, man, you doin' okay?"

"Yeah. I came by to say adios. I'm off to Vegas to live with my dad."

"Hmm." Frankie's response wasn't exactly what Nacho expected. He thought he'd say something more, like "Wow, what happened?" Or, "Hey, we're gonna miss you, dude." Instead, all he got was "hmmm."

"Yeah, my mom and dad talked it over, so I'm outta here. Vegas. I don't know much about it. Gambling, I guess, is what they do there. Desert, mostly. I saw somethin' on TV about Vegas once, but never thought I'd be livin' there. Looks hot."

"Yeah, guess so. Jaime! Jaime, are you ready to go?"

"You guys goin' someplace?"

"Yeah… Jaime, you one-eyed freak, let's get a move on. The guys are expecting us in about fifteen. Hey, Nacho, you gonna sell some weed to those white kids from Saratoga you was tellin' me about? It is there on the table for you."

"Uh, yeah. Yeah, I am. I'll do it now, then maybe we can…"

"Jaime! Jaime, c'mon! Yeah, Nacho, yeah. We'll see you later, man. Jaime, let's roll!"

Frankie didn't seem to even care!

As Nacho picked up the bag from the

table, Jaime came walking out of his room. He looked sick.

"Dude, you okay? You don't look too hot," Nacho asked.

"Huh? Yeah, I'm just kinda done in from last night. The Kool-Aid and the beers don't mix. I kept throwing up last night."

In a sharp tone, Frankie yelled at Jaime," Dude, you are such a little wimp. Sittin' here complaining about a tummy ache. Pobrecito…or should I say pobrecita?" He started laughing at Jaime, who rolled his eye at Nacho.

"Did I hear you're leaving for Vegas to live with your dad?"

Frankie heaved a big sigh, "Jaime, this ain't a time for a chat with Nacho. Yeah, he's leaving. He's leaving right now to go and sell some, so let him go and we gotta get going."

Nacho ignored Frankie's attitude, and answered Jaime.

"Yeah, I leave Thursday."

Frankie started for the door, and Jaime followed him like a dutiful puppy.

Nacho grabbed the bag and walked out with them.

"I'll leave the door unlocked for you Nacho. When you get the money, come back here and drop it off on my bed. Better yet, hold onto it and I'll pick it up from you tonight. I don't want that little thief, Carlos, getting my cash."

Jaime laughed, "Or mom"

"Yeah, or mom. She'd waste it on her drugs and boyfriends," Frankie responded.

"Sounds cool. Then I'll see you tonight. I need to stop by my house and grab somethin' first."

Frankie and Jaime left, and Nacho began to walk down the driveway when Carlos walked over. He'd been sitting on the porch the whole time listening.

"I'm coming with you, man"

"Cool, Carlos, you come with me. I'll show you the place to sell and the Saratoga kids. I gotta grab my pistol first. You wait outside." He didn't want Carlos to hear Marcella or his mom start nagging on him again.

As Nacho through the door of his house, Marcella was vacuuming. The whine of the vacuum drowned out the sound of Nacho walking to his room. He grabbed his gun that he had hidden under his mattress, and quickly walked out.

"Okay, man, let's move it down to the store. So, you heard I'm moving to Vegas, huh?"

"Yeah, man. Yeah. I'm sorry to see you leave. You're cool, man. Frankie don't seem to care, but I guess he does. He just…I dunno…sometimes he's in a big hurry to get things done. I feel sorry for Jaime sometimes. I mean, man…bein' with one eye and all. He always gets treated bad by the home boys."

"Yeah, I know. Jaime's a good man. You got two good brothers there, Carlos. Take care of them and they take care of you. Family is important, and that means your home boys, too."

When they arrived at the store, Nacho and Carlos took their spot by the bushes on the side of the store. They waited for awhile. Carlos picked up a couple of sticks and was scratching gang symbols in the dry dirt around the bushes, .".so everybody knows this is our piece," he said. Nacho grinned and nodded his head in agreement.

The car appeared in the parking lot and slowly made its way to where they stood.

"This them?" Calos asked.

Nacho nodded, then picked his chin up and walked over to where the car parked.

"Hey, esse!" the driver said.

"Esse? Esse? Who this white boy callin' 'esse'? You ain't one of us. You don't go callin' us 'esse'" Carlos yelled out with an attitude.

"Whoa, little dude. Who's this little man you got with you, your body guard?" the driver asked Nacho.

"No, he's the man you be dealing with from now on. I'm movin' to Vegas where there's better action. So, you want the same as last time?"

The boy on the passenger side lowered

his head so he could look out the driver's window. "So, you the one who sold us the stuff last time?"

"Yeah. Why?"

"That was some good stuff, man. Fine, real fine. My compliments to the chef!" The two other boys in the backseat of the car laughed.

"Well?" Nacho asked, thinking about the cash.

"Well, what? Oh, yeah, the money. You want your money. Let's see what we're buying," the driver said.

Nacho held the bag while the driver peeked in. He fingered the weed a bit, and dug through it.

"This ain't an ounce"

"Yeah it is"

"No, it ain't. I said I wanted an ounce, and this sure doesn't look like an ounce, ess...," he cut short of saying the word as he looked at Carlos. Carlos was glaring at him. "This just doesn't look right."

"Thirty bucks. I'm giving you thirty cuz I

think you're shorting us."

"Its forty, or no deal. I told you it's an ounce. It's an ounce." Nacho started getting tense, and he knew they could feel it, too. His face became solid, like it was made of stone. Cold stone. His eyes fixed on the driver, and his left hand slid down to his pistol enough that the bulge of the pistol under his tee shirt began to bulge.

"Its looks like an ounce to me. Yeah, I do believe it is an ounce," said the kid on the passenger side.

"Damn right it's an ounce, esse," quipped Carlos. "You know what? The price is gonna start going up pretty soon, too, if you don't make a decision. It's called 'inflashun'."

One of the kids in the back seat laughed. "That's some kid you got there, man."

"I ain't no kid. I woop your stupid white a…" Nacho cut Carlos short of the rest of the threat.

"We got a deal or not? I'm busy."

"Yeah. Yeah, we got a deal. I'm not happy about this, but we got a deal. Next time, let's see more. Okay?"

Nacho looked at Carlos. "You heard the man, more the next time."

Carlos nodded in agreement. "I still think the price might go up cuz of their attitude, but I'm treat 'em right, Nacho."

The driver slipped the money into Nacho's hand as Nacho slipped the bag into his. As the car drove away, Nacho looked at Carlos and smiled.

"Man, you got what it takes. You know your stuff, dude. Good!"

"I still think we coulda got more than forty. We coulda got another five from them and bought some food."

"Yeah, maybe, but you gotta remember when a deal is being made and the question is asked if you got a deal, the first person to speak looses. Ask the question, then let them answer; otherwise, you could blow a deal off quick. Remember that, okay?"

"Okay. Man, those white kids actin' like their all that. Who they think they are, man? Like they be from the streets an' all. They ain't nothin' but a bunch of rich kids treatin' us like dirt. Like dirt, Nacho. They actin' like they's better than us."

"Money. That's what it's all about, Carlos. Money. They gots money to blow cuz they gots dads and moms who gives them money so's they don't hafta be with 'em. Their dads and moms, they rich. Richer than any of us. They's got big homes, fancy pools, fancy cars, but they ain't much different than us. Those kids, they hangin with their home boys, too. Just, they richer than us."

"Yeah, maybe so. But, seems to me they got an attitude. Like, 'hey, we better'n you. You see that kid in the back seat of the car? He was wearin' a watch that cost, man. Someday, someday I gonna have a watch like that. And, and, I gonna drive a big fancy car and look down on people."

Nacho laughed, "Hope so, Carlos, hope so. When you do, you come lookin' for me and share some of that. Sound okay?"

"You got a deal, man."

That night, Nacho partied hard. He

partied with Tony, Frankie, and the other guys. He told them about how Carlos handled himself, and how the deal went. They drank and smoked until dawn. Nacho got home, and went into his room. His suitcase was there, but things were different. His mom and Marcella had thrown out a lot of his stuff. He flopped onto his bed to sleep off his night.

The next day was quiet. Hungover, Nacho sat on the couch and watched TV. His head pounded, and he was thirsty. He drank water, but it never seemed to be enough. He looked in the kitchen, but there was only a half bag of chips, some bologna, peanut butter, and a few tortillas. He smeared peanut butter on the tortilla and rolled the chips and bologna in it. He took big bites, and had it finished faster than it took time to make it. He went back into his room, and slept some more.

When he came back out of his room again, the house was dark. His mom and Marcella were sleeping. He glanced at the clock in the kitchen and saw that it was four in the morning. He had slept his entire day away.

"Nacho, are you in there? Nacho?" Marcella's voice cut through the door like a knife.

"Yeah, what?"

"It's time. Time for us to take you to the airport. We got a taxi outside waitin'. So, hurry up, the time is costin' us."
He grabbed his suitcase, and hurried into the bathroom. He washed his face and used the toilet. He quickly ran back into his bedroom and grabbed his old sweatshirt. He stuffed it into the suitcase.

Marcella looked at him with repugnance. "Great. You stink like you've been partying all night. Why didn't you shower? I feel sorry for the people sittin' next to you on the plane."

His mom was already sitting in the taxi talking to the driver. As Nacho walked out of the door, he saw the old man across the street. He stood still, staring at Nacho. Nacho tossed his suitcase into the open trunk of the taxi, closed it, and got in.

The driver didn't turn around, but looked at Nacho through the rearview mirror.

"Airport?"

"Yeah, I guess so."

The drive didn't take but a few minutes, and his mom was quiet during the entire ride.

Once there, the driver got out and took the suitcase out of the trunk.

"Your mother handled the tip already, son."

"Oh, yeah, okay."

His mother got out of the taxi and stepped up to Nacho to give him a hug and a kiss. "Mico, I'm going to miss you. You keep in touch, okay? You call if you need anything. I love you."

"I love you, too. Mom, I really do."

"Here are your tickets. They'll give you the boarding pass. Be sure to check the board and be sure you're at the right gate. And, remember to…" Embarrassed, Nacho looked at the taxi driver.

"Mom, I'm okay. I know what to do."

Entering into the airport, the faint smells of jet fuel blended with the scent of perfume and coffee. Airports have an odor that is unique, and the odor reminded Nacho of when he and his mom returned home after the accident at Disneyland. The flood of memories flushed into his mind, and the thought of that time carried an odd feeling. He checked his luggage, and found his way to the gate. Standing in line to board the plane for Vegas, he noticed people looking at him. Some turned away as soon as he caught their eyes. He made sure his bandana was on. As they boarded, he found his seat and prepared for takeoff.

"Ladies and gentlemen, the Captain has turned on the Fasten Seat Belt sign. If you haven't already done so, please stow your carry-on luggage underneath the seat in front of you or in an overhead bin. Please take your seat and fasten your seat belt. And also make sure your seat back and folding trays are in their full upright position."

There was an excitement on the plane; there always is. Nacho was seated along the aisle, near the back.

"If you are seated next to an emergency exit, please read carefully the special instructions card located by your seat. If you do not wish to perform the functions described in the event of an emergency, please ask a flight attendant to reseat you."

Nacho looked around and saw people still finding their seats. As the announcements continued, Nacho looked at the magazine in the pocket in front of him. It was filled with pictures of flights and places he knew he'd never see.

"Now we request your full attention as the flight attendants demonstrate the safety features of this aircraft." He knew the drill; he'd seen it before even on TV. "Flight attendants, prepare for take-off please." As the plane taxied out to the runway, Nacho could feel the power of the engines. Suddenly, there was a surge as the plane began picking up speed. He could feel the plane's nose rise, and finally the entire plane lift off the ground. He was up. People were looking out the windows at California's great Central Valley below. Within minutes, they were over the towering sierra range. He could feel the plane making a descent; "the flight was so short for the distance they'd covered," he thought.

The captain's voce came across the loudspeaker, "Flight attendants, prepare for landing please." Nacho took a quick glance out of the window. The sprawling city below seemed oddly placed, almost like it was a toy city stuck in the middle of the desert. He could see the casinos. Cars moved about like little ants. As the plane began to touch ground, he felt the bump and heard the brakes.

"Ladies and gentlemen, welcome to McCarran International Airport, Las Vegas, Nevada. Local time is ten fifteen and the temperature is a pleasant ninety degrees. For your safety and comfort, we ask that you please remain seated with your seat belt fastened until the captain turns off the Fasten Seat Belt sign. This will indicate that we have parked at the gate and that it is safe for you to move about." People didn't seem to care, as soon as the place stopped moving, people were getting up and grabbing things in the overhead bins.

People jammed the narrow aisle, and Nacho struggled to stand up. He cut into the line in front of a woman who appeared to be in her forties.

"Oh, my gosh. Some people, I tell you...," she said looking at a person seated to her right.

Nacho ignored her complaints and pushed forward. Exiting the plane and walking out into the terminal, he saw Marcello. He had a big smile on his face, and quickly walked up to Nacho.

"I'm glad to see you, son. I love you. I really do. It is so good to have you here."

Nacho was taken back. Was this the same man who he was ready to shoot? This was the same guy who beat his mom, got drunk, and was wasted all the time?

"Hey, dad. Good to see you too."

"Your flight, it was good?"

"Yeah. Short, but good."

"Did you have anything to eat? Are you hungry? Let's grab your bags and go get something to eat, okay? Good to see you. I am so sorry, you know, about the way things went, but things are going to be different between us, you'll see." The rush of words from Marcello's mouth bombarded Nacho. This was not what he expected, and Marcello was actually a nice guy!

They went to the carousel and waited for Nacho's suitcase. "Things, Nacho, things haven't always been right between us. I ain't gonna lie. I haven't been the dad you expected. So, things are different. I'm different. We'll be getting' a fresh start."

"Okay, sounds good to me," Nacho answered. "Hey, there it is."

"I'll grab it for you. Is that all you brought? You just had one suitcase?"

"Just one. That's it."

"Okay, ummm..well..it will work okay. We'll get you set up with more stuff later. Let's get something to eat."

As they sat down in a small diner and had sandwich, the two of them spoke; but, Marcello did most of the talking. He spoke of Las Vegas, the heat, the people, and how he wanted a different life for Nacho. They drove over to Marcello's apartment, and walked inside. Nacho could smell the lingering smell of pot, bacon, and coffee. He put his suitcase down by the couch, and sat down in the chair at the kitchen table. Marcello walked over to a closet and opened it up. On the shelves were kilos of weed, and bags of various drugs. He grabbed a bag on placed it on the table in front of Nacho.

"Well, what do ya' think? Huh? We got a business here, and I have us set up for some big time dealin'. We can make a lot of money here in Vegas. The people, here, are really doin' it and spend some big cash for it. We got it made, son. We got it made!"

Nacho sat, motionless. He didn't know what to say. Here he was stuck in Vegas, and this is what it was all about?

"Dad, I…I thought things was gonna be…like…different."

"What ? Whatch'a mean? This is it! Right here, now. We got things to do, so let's get rolling out there and make some deals."

They got into Marcello's car and drove to various parts of Las Vegas, where Marcello was known. There were some restaurants where Marcello drove up in the back alleys and dealt. There were a couple of parks, where they drove and made deals. The entire rest of the day was spent dealing, and Marcello had about a thousand dollars on him by the end of the day. They went out and had dinner at a steakhouse, and then returned to Marcello's apartment.

"Tomorrow, we got a big deal going down. It's in a park, and there are some regulars there who want a kilo. So, we're heading over there tomorrow. You sleep here, on the couch for now. We'll get you set up later."

Nacho was in a daze. The whole day was one, big blur. Nothing made any sense. His head was swimming from the experience. He flew into Vegas, ate, and then was dealing all in one day? He was exhausted emotionally and physically. When he put his head down on the couch pillow, he fell asleep almost instantly. He was done in.

The sound of the bathroom shower woke him up the next morning. Marcello was in the bathroom, and Nacho was lying there looking at the ceiling. The popcorn ceiling was stained with the tar and nicotine. There were cobwebs in the corners, and a small fly was buzzing around in the kitchen. He turned and lifted his head to look in the kitchen. Three small pots and a couple of dirty dishes were sitting on the counter with dried food on them. "Not like home," he thought to himself. "Mom would never let things go like that."

"You up? Hungry? I can whip up somethin' for us to eat if you're hungry. I bet you are." Marcello came walking out of the bathroom wearing his shorts. Nacho saw the track marks on his dad's arms and legs.

"Let's see here. Yeah, I got some puffed up wheat cereal here. Milk. Hmmm...I ain't got any milk." Marcello looked in the cupboard and took out some packets of coffee creamer he had taken from a restaurant. He opened them up and dumped the contents into a glass, put some tap water in, placed his hand over the glass, and shook it. "There. Now we got milk," he chuckled. Grabbing a blue plastic bowl from the sink, he rinsed it out and poured in some cereal. He poured the creamer on it, and then took a couple of sugar packets and sprinkled the contents on it. "A spoon. Hmm…where is a spoon. Ah, yes, here we go." Nacho watched as Marcello took a plastic spoon out of the drawer, wiped in off on his shirt, and put it in the bowl. "There you go. Breakfast! There's more if you want some. I'm gonna go get dressed. We gotta get going again."

As Nacho ate the cereal, he noticed it was stale. The creamer did little to improve the taste. On the lip of the bowl, there was brown stuff stuck on it. "Wonder what that is. Maybe I don't wanna know," he thought.

Calling from the bedroom, Marcello said loudly, "You sure are quiet, Nacho. You okay?"

"Oh, yeah," he answered with a mouthful of cereal. "I guess I'm still tired."

"Oh, yeah, well…you'll get yourself back in no time. Ready to roll?"

"Yeah, let me go to the bathroom first. Then we can go."

"Okay. Hey, there's a towel in there for you. It's hanging over the toilet."

Nacho got up form the couch and opened his suitcase. The few clothes he had were crumpled up and wrinkled. He grabbed a pair of pants, a tee shirt, and some socks. They smelled of mom's laundry. "She must've washed 'em for me. Hmm. and walked into the bathroom. The white walls were still moist from Marcello's shower, and the steamy air seemed still. He used the toilet, and flushed it. The toilet bowl was marked around the edges with dried urine. Out of curiosity, he lifted the lid to the toilet tak. Sure enough, there was a small baggie of pills tightly sealed and taped to the underside of the lid. When he went to wash his hands, he noticed the brown stains from hard water and dried toothpaste. The sliver of soap was the kind from hotels.

"Okay, dad, let's go." As he walked out,

Marcello had opened Nacho's suitcase. He was looking into it as though he was searching for something.

"Nice. You didn't bring any money with you, huh?"

"Just a little. I don't have much."

"Hmm. Well, we'll get that changed."

They ran down the outside stairs to Marcello's car and drove over to the park.

"Kinda reminds me of San Jose in a way," Nacho remarked.

"Yeah, sorta. Cleaner, though. Hotter, too. You'll like it here. Your mom okay?

"Yeah. Marcella's there now."

"Oh, yeah? What about Rachel?"

"Never see her. She don't come around much. She does her thing…whatever that is."

A car drove up to the park, and a couple of guys got out.

"Okay, that's them. This is pretty simple, Nacho. Come with me."

Marcello grabbed the kilo and Nacho followed him over to the guys. They were bigger than Nacho, and seemed to be 'professional' in some strange way. One had a big moustache; the other was bald and stocky.

"Here you go. Just like you ordered," Marcello said.

The bald guy looked at the kilo. "This ain't what we ordered. I told you, two kilos. Two kilos, and you was gonna give us a discount on that price because of the amount. Now, what's this? You trying to get more out of us, and make us take another visit to your park?"

"No, you said one. You said one kilo regular price and one kilo in two days," Marcello answered.

The two started arguing, and Nacho noticed the mustached man was staring at him. As the argument got louder, the swearing picked up. Nacho looked at Marcello, and saw that he had a pistol. A quickly as Nacho had noticed that, Marcello pulled it out and shot the bald guy. A splash of blood stained the man's shirt as he staggered backwards.

"Whoa. Hey! ," the mustached man said looking over at a patrol car that had just pulled up.

"Quick, Nacho, take these," Marcello said handing the pistol and kilo over. "Run!"

And run he did. Nacho ran, carrying the kilo and pistol.

"Stop! Drop the weapon. DROP IT!"

An officer was no more than 10 yards behind Nacho. Nacho stopped, dropped the pistol and kilo, and started feeling dizzy.

"Hands in the air, high. Higher! Step away from the weapon. DO IT, NOW!"

Nacho slowly stepped away.

"On your knees, NOW!"

Nacho dropped to his knees and felt nauseous. The next thing he knew, he was face down in the dirt. The officer had his knee on Nacho's back, and was cuffing him.

The officer began telling Nacho his rights, "Tiene el derecho a permanecer callado. Totdo lo…"

"I speak English, man. I know. You can tell 'em to me in English. Ow, man you're hurting my arm!"

"You have the right to remain silent.

Anything you say can and will be used against you in a court of law. You have the right to be speak to an attorney, and to have an attorney present during any questioning. If you cannot afford a lawyer, one will be provided for you at government expense. Did you understand what I just told you?"

"Dude, you're hurting my arm, man! C'mon get off me!"

"Did you understand what I just told you!"

"yeah, yeah, man, Yeah. I understood you. Just get off me, man!"

The officer picked Nacho up by his arms, and the pain in his shoulders felt like his arms were coming out of their sockets. As the officer led Nacho over to the patrol car, Nacho glanced over to see where Marcello was. He was standing off in a distance, behind a tree, pointing and laughing at Nacho. That was the last time he ever saw Marcello.

Upon arrival, the booking process at county jail took a few minutes. Nacho looked at his surroundings. Things were different here.

"What are you doing, casing the joint? Just do what we tell you, and you'll be a cell in no time." An officer started to take down all of Nacho said on a form, and then the officer gave him two pieces of paper. Nacho looked at the first one. It was an explanation of the charges and the amount of his bond.

"Listen to me, Ignacio, this other piece of paper is very important. Here is a number. This is your way to make a phone call on the inmate phone that is located in the cell block. Don't lose this piece of paper. Don't let any other inmate have it or see it. If they do, they can use your Phone Call ID Number. Do you understand me, son?"

The officer led him to a room, where there was a camera. "Face forward."
FLASH.
"Okay, turn right." Nacho was confused and scared. He turned.
"No, the other right, stupid."
"Oh, sorry. I didn't…"
FLASH

Next, they took him to the fingerprinting counter. The officer rolled Nacho's fingers into an ink pad and then onto a card. Finally, he was led into an office.

"Sit down here a minute. The nurse will be in shortly."

In less than a minute, a nurse walked in with a clipboard, and started asking questions. Nacho was afraid they'd do some kind of strip search. After all, he'd heard about that sort of thing. She asked him about his medical history, possible diseases, and his drug use. The nurse took out a small syringe from a box.

"I'm giving you a TB test. This won't hurt at all. I'll check on you in a week." Her voice was kind, and she spoke the first kind words he had heard in a long time. Somehow, they were comforting.

"Okay, Ignacio, I am now going to draw some blood. We need to do this to check for diseases." She opened a small packet of alcohol wipe and swabbed a spot on his arm, and then wrapped a rubber strap around his upper arm while telling him to squeeze a rubber ball. As he did, she located a vein in his arm and inserted a syringe. It filled with blood. As she withdrew the syringe, she quickly covered it with cotton and tape.

"Wait here a minute."

"Okay."

As he sat there waiting, he couldn't believe this was happening to him. What was going to happen? Just then, an officer entered the room.

"Stand up, Ignacio. You are going to get a fifteen minute free call. Do you know someone to call?

"My mom."

"Do you remember her number?"

"Umm..yeah, I think so...I am kinda confused here, I..."

"It happens, Ignacio. Just wait a second and try to remember her number. Calm down. Take a deep breath. Relax. Think of the number."

"Okay, yeah, I remember."

"Good, why don't you write it down here on this scrap of paper just in case you forget between here and the phone, okay?"

"Yeah, okay."

Dialing his mom was difficult to do. What would she say? When he heard the phone ringing at his home, he could imagine what the house looked like.

"Hello?" It was his mom!

"Mom?"

"Mico? Mico, where are you? What is going on?"

"Mom, I've been arrested. I'm at the county jail here in Vegas."

"What? Mico you just got there?"

Nacho could hear Marcella's voice in the background asking what was going on.

"Marcella, be quiet, please. I'm trying to talk to Nacho. He's in jail."

"What? What a stupid…"

"Marcella, please…go on, Mico, what is going on?"

"Mom, I only go fifteen minutes to talk to you. So, please tell Marcella stop! It was so confusing, mom. Dad and me were at a park and dad got into a fight with some guys and he told me to run, and I ran and got caught."

"Mico, this is not the full story. You're leaving things out. Let me see what I can do. So, what jail? Where are you?

"County jail, mom. I've been booked. They're putting me in a cell."
His mother started crying.

"Mom, please, listen…please. I didn't do nothin'. I didn't. Really. This isn't like it seems."

"Mico, Mico, Mico…my little Mico. Why do you do this to me? To yourself? Oh, Mico…." Her crying was getting worse, and Nacho didn't know what to say.
He tried to calm her down and explain, but the officer walked over and told him his time was nearly up.

"Mom, I love you. You gotta help me. Okay? Please?"

"I love you, Mico. I do. Let me see what I can do."
As he was led to his cell, where they took his shoes and gave him a pair of flip flops to wear. The realization of what had happened hit him.

He was in jail. Marcello was out, and probably didn't care. "Probably thought this would make a 'man' out of me. Stupid. Stupid, the way things are going. Well, okay. I am a home boy, so I will let people know right now they don't mess with me."

He sat in his cell for a day. Dinner was pea soup, a turkey sandwich, and an apple.

The next morning, a guard called to Nacho through the cell bars. "Pizano, we're moving you to juvie."

"Really?"

"Yeah, you're too young to be in here. You're being transferred now. Stand back while I open the door."

Nacho stood against the back wall, and the cell door opened. He was cuffed, led down the cell block to an elevator, and then he got into a car in the basement of the county jail. The ride didn't take long, but Nacho thought it was cool. When the car stopped at a stop light, he looked out the side window. A car pulled up next to him. Some girls, probably in their twenties, were looking at him. They were blonde, tan, and beautiful. Their car was nice, and they looked fine. He nodded to them, and the driver girl in the seat behind the driver nodded back and blew him a kiss. Then, the girls started to giggle and were saying things; but, he couldn't hear them. Nacho looked down at the floor of the car and noticed how clean the car was. He looked back up and over at the girls. They were laughing even harder, and one was making a face at him…mocking him. He turned and looked straight ahead.

"Gonna be awhile for you, son. You won't be seeing any pretty girls for awhile," the officer said.

"Yeah, probably."

"So, what's it like there at Juvie?"

"When we get there, you'll find out. I don't want to ruin the surprise for you," he chuckled.

Once the car arrived at the Juvenile Hall, Nacho was led out and placed into the area for teenagers. The place was cold. So cold, that he had a difficult time staying warm, which he thought was odd since this was in Vegas. But, there he was, fourteen, stuck behind concrete walls. He was led to a cell and told he could wear nothing but what they issued him. His cell has large enough to house a couple other guys. His bunk was a broken down piece of metal with a small drawer under the cot. Besides that, he had a small locker for his stuff, what stuff he had. The lock was broken, so there was no privacy. Every day was the same. He got three meals a day, two snacks, one hour of P.E. and school five days a week. Guards barked out orders constantly.

"Tuck in your shirts."

"Pull up your pants."

"Get in line."

"Stop talking."

No privacy, not even in the toilet. The toilets were communal, so everyone could see what was happening. Being watched all the time, Nacho began to feel like things were closing I on him. Kids came in; kids went out. No one cared about anyone else. It was boring, and Nacho was tired of it. School was boring.

Weekends were boring. TV and cards was an everyday thing. He felt himself wasting away. The first month passed, and no one came to see him. The second month passed, and no one came to see him. He got phone calls from his mom, but there was little either of them could say. At last, he got some news.

"Nacho," the guard said," your mom is here to take you back to San Jose. You have to go register with your probation office within five days upon arrival in San Jose. You understand?"

"Yes, sir. My mom? She's here? Now?"

"Yes, she is in the waiting area, so clean out your locker. Here's a bag. I'll be back in a minute to take you to the office. We'll have your discharge papers ready for you and your mom."

Nacho took the bag and dumped everything he had into it. There wasn't much, so it hardly took any time. Then, he waited. He sat on his cot and waited. It seemed like forever, but it was only fifteen minutes or so.

"Okay, buddy, let's go," said the officer.

They walked to the office and his mother was waiting for him. She was seated in a chair, holding her purse. She looked like she'd been crying. When he came through the door, she stood up and gave him a hug.

"Mico, Mico! My Mico! You're going home. Yes, home. We're flying home to San Jose. Now, you can start fresh, okay?"

The officer had a blank expression on his face. No emotion.

"Mrs. Pizano, there are some forms for you to sign. She looked at the forms as the officer described what they were about. This form clearly states you and your son will meet with the probation officer in San Jose within five days. Do you understand, mam? This must be done."

"Yes, oh yes. Thank you, officer. We will. My son will turn his life around, you'll see, he will! Right, Mico? Right?"

The officer still had no emotion, just an authoritative air.

"I hope so, mam. For both your sakes, I hope

so. You've got a good mother here. I hope you listen to here and stop doing the stupid stuff you're doing. Otherwise, you'll be back in a place like this or worse. You understand me?"

"Yes."

"'Yes', what?"

"Yes, sir."

Nacho's mom looked at him is disbelief. He was showing some respect? Nacho and his mom got into a taxi and headed for the airport. As he sat back in the seat, he listened to the words…

"Flight attendants, prepare for take-off please." Nacho could feel the power of the engines, and he recalled that feeling he had just two months before. Only two months? Had it been two months? It seemed like it had been a year. The surge as the plane began picking up speed was exhilarating. He was up, away from Vegas, and heading home.

IX
The Streets Call

"Mico, it is so good to have you home again. I know things will be better for you. Tomorrow, we go to the probation office, okay? Then, we get some clean clothes for you since you left everything at Marcello's. Everything will be different for you now."

Nacho looked around. The house, clean and fresh, was welcoming. Mom had cleaned the house for his arrival. He walked into his room. His bed was nicely made for him. The walls were bare, and the room had been aired out. His mom had put an Air-Wick in the room to cover the stale odors.

"So, you're home. Things are going to be different, right?" Marcella had walked into the room and was standing at the bedroom door. There was a demanding tone in her voice.

"Yeah, different."

"Well, we'll see. We'll see. I want to see some changes, Nacho. Seriously. Mom and me talked a lot while you were...hmm...away," she sneered. "I expect some changes. Mom doesn't need this, you know."

"Marcella? Marcella! Come here," Nacho's mom yelled. "Come here, please. I want you to leave Nacho alone. Stop nagging him. Things are going to be different. God has plans for Nacho. You'll see. Big plans. Now, he is on the right path."

Before she left the room, Marcella leaned in towards Nacho and said,"Mom has big hopes for you. Don't disappoint her."

Nacho looked around in his dresser. There were some of his clothes there, and one of his old bandanas was there. He put it on.

"Mom, I'm going out."

"Okay, Mico, but please be careful. I trust you to be careful."

"I will."

He headed over to Frankie's house. Jaime and Carlos were there, but Frankie was gone.

"HEY! Look who is back, man! Look at

you, home boy! You lookin' like you gained some weight," said Jaime with a smile.

"Hey homes. Hey Carlos. So, like what's been happenin' while I been locked up?"

"The same ol, same ol'. Good to see you, man, like its been two months and we haven't heard anything 'cept you was locked up in Vegas."

"Yeah, pretty much it."

"I'm going over to the store to sell some weed. Wanna come? I gots a little bit to sell to those Saratoga kids, and then there's a man who comes by to get some," said Carlos, "I could use you."

"Sure, esse, I'm with ya'."

Jaime stood back. "You guys go ahead, I'm stayin' here. I think Tony is coming by later, and we're pickin' up beer for a party. Hey, let's celebrate you comin' back, homes."

"Sounds good to me. I'm there already! Tell Frankie I'm back."

Carlos had already started walking down the street, and Nacho caught up to him.

"See what I got? I got me a watch kinda like that kid we saw in the car, 'cept it ain't expensive. Looks like it, though. Looks like a rolodex, just like he got."

"I think you mean Rolex. Rolodex is one of them office card flippy things. Rolex is the watch."

"Yeah, yeah, Rolex. Like a fancy watch like those rich kids have. Cool, huh? It keeps time pretty good, too. I go to school and the girls think I gots a Rolod…I mean, Rolex watch."

"You goin' to school? Cool, Carlos. Cool. A brother of mine told me to go to school, that it is important, but I didn't listen to him. You should. You're smart. You can do it."

"Yeah, yeah…I get some good food there at least. I gots friends there, too. I wanna be rich. I figure I can do this until I gets enough money to go and get to be something better. Yeah, man, better. I wanna be somebody. They had a speaker at the school last week at an assembly. He said, 'You can be what yu wanna be, keep your dream alive'"

Nacho smiled as he looked at Carlos. "You got a dream, man?"

"Yeah, sure do. I watched a program on TV. They was talkin' about rich and famous people. Some guy with an accent was holding a glass of wine, and talking about how the rich and famous people live. Someday, that'll be me. Rich and famous."

When they got to the store, the 'Saratoga car' drove up.

"So, you back in town?," asked the driver.

"Yeah, but this is his business," Nacho said, pointing to Carlos.

"Okay, Mr. Businessman, what you got for me today?"

"The usual."

"Okay, and the usual price?"

"That's right."

Nacho watched as the kid slipped a fifity dollar bill into Carlos's hand and took the bag. As the car drove off, Nacho's eyebrows went up and he looked at Carlos.

"So, Mr. Businessman, the price of weed suddenly went up?"

Carlos had a big grin, "It's called 'inflashun'. We got one more who comes by here. He's a rich dude from Los Gatos. Got lots of money. He saw my watch, and said it looked really fine." About ten minutes later, a black Jaguar drove up. The driver side window went down, and a hand came out with two twenty dollar bills. Carlos handed the man an ounce of weed. Nacho noticed the man wore a nice coat with a white shirt. The gold cufflinks with a diamond sparkled. The man said nothing; just did the deal and drove off.

"What happened to 'inflashun'? He don't have to worry?"

"Heck, no. He say someday he gonna let me take a ride in that fine car of his and let me see how the rich and famous live. Way I figure it, man, you gotta take care of those who gonna take care of you."

When they got back to the house, Frankie had his car ready to go. Polished and cleaned up, it was a sweet ride. Frankie,

Jaime, Tony, Carlos, and Nacho piled into the car and went for a ride. First, they stopped off at Mark's Hotdogs and had their fill. Then, they took a ride over to a guy's house who Nacho hadn't met before. There was plenty of beer, and soon it was like old times. Nacho was smoking weed and drinking beers. The music was on, and things were as though nothing had happened in Vegas. Nacho told them about the county jail, being booked, and how the Juvenile Hall was.

"Man, you are so in. You been in the joint already. You are a true home boy, dude. True soldier, forever," said one of the guys.

"Yeah, you is one of the soldiers of the streets," said another.
Nacho sat back on the couch. Yes, he was one of the true soldiers of the streets.

"So, like if you was gonna die, Nacho. If you was gonna die, how would you go? For real," said one of the older guys.

"Like a soldier. I would stare them square in the eyes, man. Wearing my colors, and lettin' them know how much I hate 'em all."

"Yeah, man, yeah! That's what I'm talkin' about right there. That man, right there. He got what it takes. Right there," yelled a large guy with tats all over his arm.

Nacho looked over the man, and asked Jaime, "who is that?"

"Dude, he is like the leader of La Ganga, dude. He is THE man. If you commit to La Ganga, you under him."

The man walked over to Nacho. "When you are ready, we can use a man like you. You got what it takes, dude. You do."

As the evening wore on, Nacho thought about what the man had said about committing. He could do it.

"Hey, Nacho, Tony is going back home. You wanna ride?"

"Yeah, I better go. I gotta meet with someone tomorrow."

X
Recall

Nacho got up early and showered, so he'd make a good impression on the probation officer. After he showered, he put on some clean clothes and left his bandana behind.

"You clean up very nicely, when you want to," said Marcella.

"Thanks"

"So, out partying it up with your home boys?"

"Maybe, but I don't see how that can be any of your business."

"As long as you don't make it my business, we're okay."

"I'm ready to go," Nacho's mom said as she walked into the living room. She smelled nice with her perfume.

"Let's go."

Marcella had her own car, and so she drove them to the Probation Department. As she was driving, Marcella asked, "Mom, are you ever going to get a driver's license?"

"No."

"Why?"

"Don't need it."

"Why?"

"Cuz you got one."

"Oookay, so I guess that answers that question."

They all laughed.

Marcella looked in the rearview mirror at Nacho. "What about you, Nacho?"

"Maybe. We'll see how things work out."

Nacho's meeting with the probation officer went by quickly as he outlined the process. They were home within a couple of hours, and Nacho decided to go over to Tony's. He'd seen Tony's car parked outside, and thought a visit would be good. The visit with Tony became an all night hangout, and Nacho was soon sitting in the park with the gang. They were drinking beer and relaxing. A patrol car came up and one of the officers walked over to the group. Nacho quickly grabbed an empty soda can, and poured his beer into it.

"Hey, guys. So, are you drinking beer in the park? Some of you look pretty young to be drinking," the officer said, "how about you?" Looking at Nacho, he pointed his finger.

"Me? No, sir. Only soda."

"Hmm, right. You kinda smell like you've been drinking. Strong soda, probably."

"Yeah, soda is pretty strong stuff." As the officer walked away, the guys smiled and looked at Nacho. "They got you pegged, man," said one of the guys. "Pretty quick thinking, Nacho. Good for you."

The weeks went by, and most nights Nacho was out with his friends. Things slipped back into the same old routine. His mom was complaining about his late nights, Marcella was still on his case. Things were just like they were before he went to Las Vegas. The only difference was that now he had to check in with his probation officer, a man who was overworked and probably underpaid. His caseload was so big, Nacho wasn't a priority.

There was a knock on the door about 9:00 at night. Nacho was sitting on the couch watching TV. He got up and walked over to answer it.

"Tony, what's up?"

"Nacho, we got a situation and I need your help."

"Yeah? What's up, esse?"

"I gotta guy with a load of weed and stuff. We need to get it, now. I need you and Frankie. Frankie is in the car. You ready to ride?"

"I'm there, let's go."

They sped down the road, and went into a residential area. Tony turned off the lights and engine, letting the car coast to the front of a house. Quietly, they got out, and didn't close the doors. Frankie gave a pistol to Nacho and whispered. "We're going in, you make sure that man doesn't move a muscle. He moves; you shoot. When you shoot, shoot him in the head. Tony and me are going to get the stash. Then, we get out." They crept up to the house quietly, and Tony peeked in through a window. "Okay, he is on his couch. The TV is by the door. This is easy. We go in, turn left and he is right there. Ready…go!"

They smashed in the door, and Nacho quickly came in first. Sure enough, the man was sitting exactly where Frankie said he'd be. Nacho ran in front of the man holding the pistol out in front, directly at the man's head.

"Move, and I'll kill you now."

The man froze, staring at Nacho as the other two went into the other room.

"You don't think…," the man started to say.

"Shut up. I said don't move a muscle." There was noise in the other room as the house was being searched. The man sat there, memorizing Nacho's face. Finally, Tony and Frankie emerged carrying the stash in a bag.

"We got it. Let's go," Tony said.

Nacho stood there holding the gun in the man's face. The temptation to shoot was overwhelming.

"Dude, I said let's go!"

"I'm backing out right now. So help me, I'll drop you if you move. You hear me? I'll blow your brains all over your walls," Nacho said tensely.

"I'll remember you," the man said quietly.

"Good. You do that. You remember

me. I'll drop you if I ever see you."
Nacho backed out of the room and they ran to
the car. Tony already had the car running.
Frankie was half way to the car, and Nacho
backed out, and then ran to the car. He was
hardly in the car before they were halfway
down the street.

"Wooo! That was good! Man, Nacho, I
thought that guy was gonna piss his pants right
there. He was frozen, dude. Frozen to that
couch. If he had pissed, it would have been
comin' out as ice cubes, "said Tony. Frankie
was laughing, and Nacho was hyped up from
the experience. Tony started screaming,
"What a rush, dude!, You are crazy, man.
Crazy."

That night, they partied with a bunch of
other guys. They partied so hard, nacho was
totally wasted. They went for another ride, and
went to some other houses. They were all
over San Jose that night. When Nacho
stumbled into his house, it was almost five in
the morning. He didn't know what day it was,
and he didn't care. He went to his room and

slept.

It was three in the afternoon. The sun was hidden behind the fog, and a cool breeze was coming in from the south bay. A knock on the door woke Nacho up. He went to the door, and a few of the guys were standing there from the night before.

"Hey, dude. Hey, you need to come out here to the car. There's a girl here. She needs to talk to you."

"What, what about? I didn't touch any girl last night…not like that."

"No man, she needs to talk to you. Come on."

Nacho walked out to the car. The cool air hit his face and sobered him up a bit more. He saw a girl from the party the night before. He vaguely recognized her. She was sitting in the front seat nervously picking at her nails. It was Cecilia.

"Hey, what's up? Cecilia, what's up?"

"Nacho, you killed someone last night. Don't you know? You shot that kid, John Lopez, last night at my house. He was partying, and you shot him. The police are, like, all over the place looking for who shot him."

"Who? Who is he? I didn't even know hardly anyone there. Least, not any kid at any party last night. Who is John Lopez? What...how did I kill him?"

"You shot him, dude," one of the guys said. He was sitting down drinking a beer, and you shot him."

Nacho's stomach turned, and he ran behind the car to vomit.

"You don't even know... and you shot him? Why, Nacho? Why? I don't understand," cried Cecilia.

Nacho looked up from behind the back of the car, "I really shot him dead? Are you sure? I mean, I don't even remember it. I can't make my brain remember that. Are you sure someone else didn't do that?"

"We gotta be cool, man. Just keep it cool. Not everyone saw it, okay? Be cool. Chill for awhile," one guy said firmly.

"Yeah, yeah, yeah," repeated Nacho.

"So, my pistol? I shot him with my pistol? Where's my pistol? I don't remember anything," Nacho whispered raising his hands as if questioning. Sweat started to bead on his forehead, and he felt like he wanted to puke again.

"I'm...I'm sorry Cecilia. I mean, I dunno what to say 'cuz I can't even remember what happened. I was so wasted, I can't even remember."

"Just go back into your house and stay low awhile. Things will clear up. Just chill," said one of the other guys.

"Okay, yeah...chill...yeah...okay."

As the car drove away, Nacho walked into the house and went to the bathroom. He had the dry heaves, and felt chilled. His body didn't even feel like it was his own. "This can't be real, can it? I didn't, did I? GOD! No, I didn't, did I? This isn't real. This is a nightmare. I'll wake up. I know I will," he thought. He went to his room, and curled up on his bed in a fetal position. He heard the front door open, and then close. It was his mom.

Should he tell her? What should he do?

"Mico? Mico, are you home?"

"I'm here mom"

"Good! Do you want some dinner?"

"No, mom, no."

"Are you going out again with your friends? Please stay home, Mico."

"I'm staying home, mom. I think I will stay home for awhile. I need to be here at the house with you."

"Oh Mico, that makes me happy to hear you say that. I love you, Mico"

"Love you too, mom"

"Are you okay? Why don't you come out here and see me?"

"Umm. Okay. Mom I don't feel so good."

"Are you sick? Do you need something? I can get you something if you're not feeling well. Maybe you need something to eat."

Nacho walked out of his room. His mother looked up at him with a concerned and loving look. "Mico, you don't look too good. You caught something, perhaps."

"Yeah, I think so. I think I'll rest awhile. Okay?"

And he did rest. For the next couple of weeks, Nacho rested. He didn't leave the house except for one time to take a walk with Carlos to the store to do a deal. Frankie, Tony and Carlos knew what had happened, but no one spoke of it. It was secret, and the secret was too important. After a month, Nacho figured it was okay to start going out with his friends, but the murder hung on him like a weight. Another month passed, then it happened...

"Mico? Mico? There are some police here to see you. Mico?"

Nacho walked out of his room. He saw two officers standing at the door.

"Igancio Pizano? My name is Officer Flores. I'm with the San Jose Police Department. This is Officer Johnson. May we have a word with you for a moment?"

"Yeah, sure."

"Do you know a man by the name of John Lopez?"

"No, but the name sounds familiar."

"Were you at a party about two months ago where Mr. Lopez was?"

"Yeah, I guess. I think so. I don't remember."

His mother was standing in the room listening, "Mico, what's going on? What happened?"

"Mr. Pizano. We're placing you under arrest for the murder of John Lopez. Turn around please." As he did, Nacho felt the cuffs go on his wrists. The words once again were heard…

"You have the right to remain silent. Anything you say can and will be used against you in a court of law. You have the right to speak to an attorney, and to have an attorney present during any questioning. If you cannot afford a lawyer, one will be provided for you at government expense. Did you understand what I just told you?"

"Yes."

Nacho knew the routine. He went through the booking process just like he had before in Las Vegas. His mother went along with him as far as the police would allow, but then they had to separate. His papers were handed to him. As he walked to his cell, a man came walking up.

I'm a public defender. Hand me that paper, please."

Nacho had never done that part before. Who was this guy? He handed the papers to the man, who disappeared behind a crowd of other people. He was led to his cell. As he sat down, odors of stale smoke from cigarettes and marijuana merged with the rank stench from the toilets in the cellblock. As he sat on his bunk, he could feel the fear welling up inside him. His stomach quivered each time he heard the angry shouts of the other convicts as they challenged each other from behind their bars.

XI

Friends

Days grew into weeks for Nacho, with the routine of prison ticking away at life like a clock. Nothing changes in prison. The faces are the same, the stories are the same, and the meals are the same. Some days, however, are punctuated by events that shake the place.

"Line up. Time for breakfast. Gates opening. Line up! Put your hands in your pockets. Do it, NOW." The guard's loud voice cut through the air. The line to the chow hall seemed a bit different today. There was something 'in the air', and the men felt it. It was an uncomfortable feeling like something was about to erupt. The guards sensed it too, and seemed a bit edgy. Nacho looked up the line and saw Jaime. "Dang, that stupid kid is in here?" he thought to himself. "What did he do?"

Once he had his breakfast tray, Nacho looked around for a place to sit. There they were. Jaime was sitting at a table with the Big Man and some other guy. The other guy looked vaguely familiar- it was Tony! Only, Tony looked so thin. He didn't look like the kid down the street anymore; he was grown up. It had been awhile since he had seen him.

Nacho heard Tony was in the system, but didn't know he was here at San Quentin. Nacho found a seat at the table.

"Yo, bro. Been awhile, man." Nacho's words received little recognition from Jaime, but Tony seemed to respond.

"Hey, home boy! It has been too long. How long you been here?"

"Too long to care; too long to count," Nacho said as he started to fill his mouth with eggs.

"Yeah, I hear ya," Tony whispered.

Nacho glanced up to see the Big Man staring at Jaime, then at him. Nacho nodded, and the Big Man didn't change his expression.

"So, you remember Jaime?"

"Yup, sure do. How you doin' holmes?"

"Great," he said as he smiled at Tony, "I'm doing great!"

Suddenly, it was like old times. Jaime and Tony were talking about the days on Biscayne Way. They laughed as they spoke of eating at Mark's Hotdogs. "Man, those are the best. It's heritage, man," Jaime laughed, and "Those are part of our heritage! I could sure…Hey Nacho, remember that time you took on Tony?" Jaime chuckled as he interrupted himself in excitement. Tony winced, and then started to laugh. "Yeah, your ol' man came out to watch you whoop ass," Tony quipped.

Nacho smiled and said, "Yeah, my ol' man always came out to see me fight."

The conversation moved from topic to topic, and Nacho heard that Jaime was married and had two kids. He had ended up at San Quentin on charges of armed robbery. As Tony and Jaime spoke, Nacho noticed the Big Man slowly moved in his seat and looked at Tony. Tony gave a quick glance at the Big Man that seemed odd. He squinted a bit before he blinked, then turned to continue his conversation with Jaime. The Big Man got up from his seat, grabbed his tray, and walked away. The conversation at the table continued and was good as the three men sat there sharing stories and laughing.

"So, how is that brother of yours, Carlos?"

The table suddenly became quiet.

"Carlos? You didn't hear? Carlos. He's dead."

"Carlos? What happened, man?"

"He went to do a deal, and didn't come back. We figured he went out and partied. So, no one was lookin' for him. About a week later, there was a news report on TV about a body bein' found in a creek in Los Gatos. Some jogger smelled a dead body and figured it to be a dead dog or somethin'. They went down to see, and noticed it was a boy's body. So, the police went down and picked him up. Gunshot to the back of the head. Bein' face down like that, his face was pretty much gone. Maggots and such… hard to identify him. He didn't have no record, so no fingerprints to look for. He had his bandana on, so police thought it wasn't worth lookin' into too hard. Figured it was a gang hit. Police found a cheap knock-off of a Rolex watch sittin' a couple of feet away from his body. It was smashed, like someone stuck their shoe on it and crushed it. They finally identified him when they found an old school lunch card stuck in the mud about ten yards away from him. Police, they came by the house and talked to my mom. She cried some, but she's so wasted all the time she really didn't care."

"Man, I'm sorry to hear about Carlos. They know who did it?"

"Nah, I figure must've been one of those deals gone bad with those kids from Saratoga or Los Gatos. I mean, figuring his body was way over there. 'Rich kids, think they can treat us like we dirt', that's what Carlos used to say. He really resented that they acted so high and mighty all the time. Maybe he just mouthed off one too many times."

"No," said Tony. "No, if he was shot in back of the head that was execution. Someone took him out in that area by the creek. Had him on his knees beggin'. Least he died like a soldier of the streets. He had his colors, right homes?"

"Yeah."

"Yeah, that's what I'm talkin' about. Died like a soldier of the streets. Prob'ly some enemies did it. Made it look like someone else."

"Yeah, but why did they find his body in Los Gatos? I mean, why there? Our enemies don't run over there, do they?"

Nacho sat, listening to the conversation. He was trying to figure out Tony's way of thinking. It did sound like a gang execution, but Jaime had a point. Los Gatos?

Nacho continued," How about Frankie? He okay?"

"Well, last time I saw him, he was all strung out on smack. He's into the stuff so bad he's thin. He ain't workin', so he lives in the streets a lot. Eatin' out of trash bins. He sold that car of his. A home boy told me he saw him sittin' on the park bench eatin' some ol' burger someone threw away. He bought him a beer, but…well… Hey, can we talk about somethin' else?"

With breakfast over, they returned to their cells. Visiting hours would be soon, and Nacho had hopes his mother would be there. It had been several days since he had seen her, and a visit with her would be good.

"Pizano. You've got a visitor!" Nacho jumped to his feet. It was a visit from his mother! His day was looking even better. As he made his way to the visitor's area, he noticed Tony and Jaime were also making their way there. Tony and Jaime were still talking and obviously enjoying each other's company. For Nacho, though, it was too much like old times. Seeing his mother's smiling face once he entered the room lightened his spirits. He was behind glass, though, because of behavior. He wanted to hug his mother, but could only place his hand on the glass over hers. She spoke to him through the glass window.

"Mico, Mico, Mico, you're still my good boy, aren't you?" she whispered   quietly.

"Yeah, yeah, I am."

"Look at you! You're thinner than you were the last time. You need to eat!   Have you been reading your Bible?"

"When I can, yeah, but sometimes it gets pretty hard to do that. I can't concentrate with the noise and everything."

"Mico, even in here God is with you. You know that, don't you? God's love isn't stopped by these walls."

"Yeah, I do." Even when he said that, he wondered. "How could God be in a place like this? Why would God be here? Why would God want me?" As his mother spoke, he saw that Tony was visiting with a woman in the open visitor's area. Well dressed and professional, she looked like she might be an attorney. Tony's visit with her was brief, and when she left he walked over to where Jaime was visiting with his wife and children. Within minutes, Tony had Jaime's little girl bouncing on his lap as he spoke with Jaime's wife. Nacho couldn't hear the conversation, but it looked like they were having a good time.

"That looks like Jaime," Nacho's mother murmured. "Is that Jaime?"

"Yeah, it is. Tony is here, too. Pretty soon, we'll have the whole hood in here."

"Mico, Marcella is tired of coming here

to see you behind the glass. Why can't you do like the others so I can hold you? Why are our meetings always behind the glass?"

"There was a fight, mom. One guy died. The guy who did it ended up at Pelican bay. I was there."

Nacho's mother sat looking at him. Her hand, so warm and gentle had a strength he could feel even through the glass. As he looked at her, he noticed how tired and worn she looked.

"What is it, Mico?"

"Nothin'. I was just thinking that's all. I gotta get back in." He could feel a   thick feeling in his throat and tears starting to well up in his eyes. "Mom, I   gotta get out of here."

"I know, I know. They're working on it. The lawyers think they may have something, but I don't know. I just don't know, Mico. Hold onto your faith   in God, Mico. Hold on. God has something for you to do."
As Nacho got up to leave and started to step away, he turned around and looked at his

mother. A tear came to his eyes when he saw his mother's careworn face.

"I love you, mom."

Turning back, he walked to the door and returned to his cell. That night as he rested on his cot, he thought about what she had said about God. Could she be right? Could God be in this place?

"God," he prayed, "is you here? I need a sign that you're here. I need to know that you really are here…here, with me now. Am I supposed to do something more than rot in this stinkin' place? God, I'm here. Help me, please, God. Please help me." As he prayed, sleep overcame him. It was a deep sleep. It was a sleep unlike any he had while he was in this place.

XII
A Job

"Nacho, we're changing your job on ya. You ain't in the kitchen today; we've got you on the list for laundry."

It wasn't too surprising. Nacho expected to be changed from his job in the kitchen. The lines formed, and the men walked to their respective jobs. If anything was going to happen, it would always be at the gates. Passing through gates was tricky, and you always had to make sure you stayed with some of your homeboys. Nacho knew this, but a kid nicknamed 'Pecas' didn't. Pecas was new to the place. Short but muscular, Pecas had a clean look. He wasn't 'tatted up', and looked like he was no more than fourteen even though he was in his twenties. As they passed through, Nacho and three other Homeboys walked through the gate, but Pecas didn't. Stuck behind the gate with Enemies, he was suddenly a target.

"Watch your back Pecas! Watch your

back!" one of the other Homeboys yelled as two men from a different gang inched their way towards Pecas. In all the noise, Pecas didn't see them advancing. "Pecas, turn around!" Nacho yelled. Pecas did, and the two men smiled at him with an evil grin. The gate opened again, and Pecas slipped through with the next group. "Don't you EVER get stuck like that again, Pecas. You gotta stay with us, bro!" Nacho screamed at him. "You gotta watch all the time, bro. We always got your back."

"Thanks, man."

A guard looked over at them, and then looked away. Nacho and Pecas lowered their voices.

"Listen to me, little bro. Don't ever trust nobody in here. The man who smiles at you has two things on his mind. He's gonna either take everything you own, or he's gonna take your life." Pecas looked down in shame. "Thanks. So, I can trust you?"

"No, man. No. I ain't here to be your babysitter, man. Yous hafta watch for yourself. We watch for each other, but yous on your own, too. Don't always trust your homeboys, neither."

And that was the way it was. The guards were just as bad as the inmates.

Nacho continued, "Listen, Pecas, and listen good. The other day there was twenty of us Homeboys shootin' hoops. The guards threw in two Sorenos inta that yard with us to teach them a lesson. They was disrespectful to the guards, so the guards wanted to teach them a lesson. I threw the ball and hit one of them inta head, then we rushed them."

"Nacho, the guards? I cain't trust them either?" Pecas asked.

"Shit, bro. Theys on the take, bro. They bringin' in drugs, weapons, whatever. They ain't here to help you, little bro. A buddy of mine gots stabbed in the head. Blood drippin' down his face, another homeboy told him which guard to go to. When he gots there, the guard asked him where he was from. When he told the guard he was with us and, the guard let him through. Didn't check him or nothin'. The guard was on a the payroll. So, little bro, you be careful."

"How deep does it go?" Pecas asked. "Homeboys gots judges, District attorneys, police on the payroll, man."

Pecas wanted to know more. "Are you committed to Homeboys?"

Nacho looked at him, and examined him carefully. "No, Pecas. I was a 'sympathizer', but when the meetings started I didn't stay."

"Why not?"

"I wanted to sometimes. I wanted to run with the big dogs, but something always stopped me. I don't know, little bro. Once you commit, they own you. You never leave- not alive anyways. I didn't want to stay. I guess I knew there was something more for me to do. God wanted me for something else. God is going to take me out of here someday."

One of the guard noticed Nacho and Pecas talking.

"Shaddup! Get in line! This ain't no time for chattin, boys!"

Nacho and Pecas got into line and started walking toward the laundry room.

"Thanks, man. Thanks" Pecas

whispered.

"No problem, little bro."

The laundry room had a clean smell of bleach, soap, and warm cotton. The dryers were already running, and some of the towels were already folded. The bins were full, and there was work to do. Talking was kept to a minimum as the crew got to work.

Most of the men were just worn out, worn to the bone tired. The days seem to drag on, and work was the best way to make the minutes pass. Always having to watch your back takes a toll on a man. It keeps a man on edge, but quiet about it. Talk too much about hurting, and people will think you're weak. That makes you a target. Some work out. Some read. Most just work and watch television waiting for time to pass until the next meal. There was one man called 'Tito'. He was about thirty. He was in for life. Some said it was for killing his girlfriend while he was high, but nobody knew for sure. Tito kept to himself. He was quiet, and the others stayed away from him 'cause he wasn't right in the head. He'd be talking to himself sometimes. He'd gotten shanked twice in the yard by other gang members for wandering into their territory even when his homeboys yelled to him to get back. The guards made sport of Tito just to see if he'd yell or fight, but he didn't. One morning they found Tito in his cell. He'd taken a handful of toilet paper and swallowed it- choked himself to death. The guard that found him said his eyes and tongue were bulging, and his face had turned dark purple. He'd suffered, no doubt about it, but didn't make a noise.

The hours passed in the laundry room, and Nacho had time to think as he folded the towels. He thought about God. Could God make him as clean as these towels? If God is love, and God loved him, could God's love be found here? Could God have a plan for him that could lift him out of this place and into something greater? Surely there had to be something more for his life than this. He thought about his mother and her faith. He thought about what he would do if God could help him out of here.

"God, are you here? Are you with me? I promise I'll change. I'll do what you want. God, I am yours. Do with me as you will. I've been a soldier of the street, now I want to be a soldier for you. Nothing in my life has meant anything. It is all gone. I am here, waiting. God, can you hear me? God, can you speak to me? God, please, please give me a sign." Nacho's prayer was sincere. There had to be an answer, but where was it?

Time was up and the men started to line up for breakfast. He looked over at Pecas who, as young as he looked, had no hope for a life. This was it for Pecas. This was his life. Was this it for Nacho?

Again, it was scrambled eggs and toast for breakfast. Nacho grabbed his tray and looked around for a table. Tony was sitting at a table talking with the Big Man again. Tony's expression was serious. As Nacho walked over, Tony looked up and saw him approaching. He said something to the Big Man, and then his whole expression changed.

A big smile came across his face.

"Hey Nacho! What's up, man?"

'Not much, bro."

Sitting down, Nacho looked across at the Big Man who, for the first time, acknowledged him.

"Nacho" he said with a deep voice.

"Hey." That was all Nacho could muster as he looked at the Big Man.

Tony must have realized that the two men had never really spoken, and broke the ice.

"Nacho, this is Jorge."

Nacho's instincts told him the man was up there in the Homeboys.

"I knew your dad. Marcello and me, we used to hang together for awhile." As Jorge spoke, Nacho knew the man was probably lying. He decided to keep the conversation short.

"Oh yeah, really? Hmm."

Jorge got up from his seat and nodded to Tony.

"See ya"

"Yeah" Tony responded.

"Nacho, nice to meet you."

"Yup, me too" Nacho said with a mouthful of toast.

Tony looked at Nacho for a moment then asked, "Have you seen Jaime around?"

"No, not today. He said something about being in the yard shootin' hoops. Why?"

"Nothin', just wondering."

With breakfast done, both men got up to go to the yard. The yard was a large enclosed area made of thick bricks and a concrete base. All the men went there to shoot hoops, hang out and catch some sun, or just talk. Most of the men just hung around in groups, talking and sharing war stories. The sun hadn't broken through the bay fog, and the chill in the air was brisk and biting. Nacho went over to sit on a bench to keep warm.

"Hay Nacho, mind if I sit?" It was Pecas.

"Sure, bro. Plenty of room"

"So, how'd you get in here?"

Nacho thought for a moment. It was tough telling the stories. Bad memories flooded his mind and the chill of the air was nothing compared to the chill of the past.

"I'm in for murder, bro. I was sent to juvie when I was fifteen. But, I got   into trouble 'cause a counselor there called my mother a 'bitch', and I beat   the livin' hell out of him. Damn near killed him for that, I did."

Pecas moved in closer to listen, enthralled with the story.

"So, they moved me to county jail. Then, at the county they shipped me to California Youth Authority to see if I was suitable for CYA. They classified me as a passive aggressive, psychopathic maniac. I came back and I thought they'd send me to CYA, but the judge said no. He sent me to Vacaville State Prison"

"Crap, man, how old were you when they did that?"

"Seventeen"

A basketball came rolling over towards Nacho and Pecas. Pecas tossed it back over to the inmates.

"So, then what happened?"

"Like you know, they send you to Vacaville 'cause it's a reception center."

"Pecas smiled, "Oh yeah. The blue side for homosexuals and sick guys, green side for the rest...man, I remember the shots and stuff. They really take you through it. Worse two weeks of my life. Bein' from the streets, I never got any chances to see a doctor. That was my first time."

"Really? Sorry to hear that, bro. But, they checked you out pretty good, huh?" chuckled Nacho. "Anyways, I was a level 3 inmate. So I thought I'd be shipped to Duel Vocational Institute. But I had an incident."

"Incident? What happened at Vacaville?"

"Yeah, well. You know those hot water faucets for coffee and all? Well, I introduced a guy to the faucet."

"Huh? Why'd you do that?"
There was innocence in Pecas that Nacho liked. His face was like a little kid, and his questions showed his inexperience in life.

Nacho's heart went out to him, and he pitied that this kid would have to be in here.

"I was again the only young one there and that nobody said nothing to me. The other gangs chilling with their own, and a bunch of others there just looking at me walk in. When I got in there, my cot and locker was in the middle of the room with two other single bunks. I was surrounded by all these guys, see? I tried   to make eye contact with the other homeboys from our gang, but they just looked away when I nodded my head 'Waz up'. I had my stuff in the footlocker. I'm there, and I'm scared. I'm only seventeen. I put my stuff in my footlocker. I had my cookies from the canteen. I just wanted my cookies, and I thought I was stupid. I love cookies, and my mom used to bake cookies. I'd eat the whole tray when she baked cookies. Anyway, I went to get a cup of water to make some Kool-aid, and when I came back I all my stuff was gone. I looked around, and everybody was looking at me- some laughing, others just staring.   One big white guy all tattooed down with 666 in big writing on his chest was sittin' eating cookies and laughing... looking right at me. I felt so scared I just wanted to crawl up in a ball and cry, but I knew if I was going to make it in there I needed to do something about it. I looked at my locker and noticed he didn't take the lock. So, I sat on my bunk, and got the lock and some soap. I put it in a sock. I tied it and got ready to handle it. As I stood up and started walking toward him, it felt like it took forever. A whole lot of thoughts went through my head. I remembered a old school homie telling me don't prove your self be down about your self right there. I new what he meant , then I remembered one of the few things my dad told me was if someone takes something of yours you not only need to get   it all back but all his stuff too to keep your respect right there. I heard his voice, I swear. This guy looks at me and says 'yours is now mine'. I said to give it back, but he started laughing and looking at his friends. Then before I knew it, I was hitting him with the sock. He picked me up and   slammed me into water fountain. His head was right under the part were the hot water came out, so I pushed the button. Hot water came gushin' out all over his face. He screamed and ran to the front of the dorm. I sat   there for a second waiting for his homeboys to jump me. I realized every one from our gang was standing up ready to fight, so I got all my stuff and his too. I was so shook up; I forgot to lock my locker. Best I did, though. It was like sendin' a message to everybody in there. It was like, 'okay, who's next. I don't need to lock my stuff up'. For the next week, I was in. Everybody was cool with me. My bunk got moved to our side, but then a white guy told me the vato had snitched on me. Next thing I know, I'm in the hole catching time and being reclassified from 3 to 5… and goin' to be sent to SQ not DVI. But, I was ok with it cuz I was taking a little respect with me. When I was being transferred to SQ, I was told to get on the wall. Next thing I know, I'm looking at Charles Manson being escorted by guards."

Pecas sat there looking at Nacho for a few seconds, and then looked out into the yard. Some of the inmates were throwing hoops and laughing. The sun had started to come out, and the fog was dissipating. It looked like the day would warm up a bit. Nacho glanced up and saw Tony. He was walking towards Jaime.

"Oh shit, no!"

"What is it, Nacho?"

"No! No!" Nacho shouted as he saw Tony take a shank from under his shirt. Jaime turned, smiling at Tony. He never saw it coming.

XIII

The Challenge

For about a week, Pecas and Nacho did not speak of the death of Jaime. There was no need to discuss the issue. After all, what was done was done. No amount of talking about it could erase the fact that Tony killed Jaime. Jaime's death did shake the prison, though. Some whispered that it was a hit planned by the Enemies; some said it was the Homeboys. A few even said that the guards told Tony to do it. Whatever the case, everyone knew that death could come from any corner.

Pecas wasn't one to wait too long for anything, and he finally had to ask Nacho what the deal was. Nacho knew the question was coming. It was only a matter of time. They were both in the yard sitting together.

"I am sorry to hear that Jaime was a friend of yours, Nacho. I know what it's like to lose a friend."

Did he? Did he really know what it was like to have boyhood friends kill each other? Did he realize the betrayal that had just occurred with the death of Jaime? Perhaps, just perhaps, he was trying to show some sympathy, but that was not something you do,in prison. That is soft, and soft gets you used and killed. Besides, Pecas was just a kid...a lap baby. He didn't know enough when to keep his mouth shut.

"Thanks, man."

"What I don't understand is why, Nacho. Why did he do that while he was smiling and all?"

"Dude, I don't want to talk about that, okay? So, why don't you just shut up and go away for awhile"

Pecas stared at him for a moment in disbelief. Nacho had no reason to talk to him like that. Besides, all he was doing was showing Nacho he was a friend.

"Hey, whatever bro. Whatever. I was just trying to..."

"I know what you was trying' to do. Just leave me alone. I got a lot on my mind, and I don't need to be thinking about Jaime and Marcello."

"Marcello? Who the hell is Marcello, Nacho?"

"I meant Tony...Tony and Jaime. I don't need to be thinking about Tony and Jaime. Look, man, I got a lot on my mind, and I would just rather not think about the thing that happened"

Pecas walked away slowly, then turned.

"Nacho, you know I am here for you if you ever need to talk. You're my only friend in here." As Pecas walked away, Nacho began to realize Pecas was. He had nothing to fear from Pecas, and all Pecas ever did was listen and try to help. Still, he had to be careful.

Marcello? Why did he say his dad's name? He hadn't thought about Marcello in a long time. Why now, why did his father's name come up now of all times? Why was it his father's name always came up when there was trouble? A wave of nausea mixed with rage came of him when he thought of his father. For an instant, he could smell his father's stink, the stench of cigarettes, booze, pot, and sweat-not the sweat of a man who works, but the sour, chemical odor of a drug addict.

"Damn that man!"

"Whoa, vato, who,you talkin to?

It was J.J. A lanky, sinewy man in his 30s, JJ looked more like he was in his early 60s. His meth habit cost him his teeth. One could tell he was probably good looking as a kid, but the drugs had reduced him to looking like all those who use the drug. They all had that same piercing gaze- somewhere between being scared or ready to fight. "Spooky" is what Johnny used to call that look. With his greasy thin hair combed back, sharp features, and missing teeth, J.J. resembled the photos of the starving Dust Bowl Okies Nacho had seen in books when he was a kid. Thing was, JJ was a smart guy. He had gone to school...graduated from high school in fact. He was religious, too. Praying at every meal, JJ stood out from the rest of the men in there. Nacho liked that about him.

"Huh?," Nacho said as though he didn't hear him ask in hopes JJ would let it pass. After all, it is embarrassing when people catch you talkin' to yourself.

"Come on, Nacho, it isn't everyday you find a guy standing alone cussing and damning someone who ain't there. Dude, it is sort of freaky if you ask me. So, who did you just decide to send to hell?"

Nacho laughed. The way JJ put it, it did seem sort of stupid.

"I was thinking about me ol man. He was something else. "

"Way I see it you don't have to turnout like your old man. He must've done something pretty hurtful for you to be damning him still. Yes, sir...pretty hurtful. So, how long you figure on letting him continue hurting you and you damning him?" JJ stood there, grinning toothlessly.

"You done being a psychologist, JJ?," Nacho flashed back.

"Dang, you a regular pissed off dude today! F-you, too."

JJ didn't swear, even though he probably used to. Still, he would say 'F' or 'BS' and such figuring that those he spoke to could fill in the blanks for him. "it weren't cussing and swearing if you don't say the words" JJ would say trying to justify his actions.

JJ walked away mumbling to himself.

Nacho realized he was angry. He had rage, and that was eating him. He was becoming like those he first saw when he came to this place. His anger was oozing out of him. Like those he saw and heard when he first came into this place, he, too, was shouting at phantoms. His loss of freedom had the walls closing in on him and, like a dog at the pound, he was starting to bite at those near him. As he looked down at his hands, he realized his fingernails were bitten down to the cuticle, and were red. Skin was torn or bitten off around the corners of what remained of the nails. He wondered, for the first time in his life, what was eating him? Was he eating himself? What would drive a man to devour himself this way? Why would a man feast on himself, and shove others away like hyenas do when when they are tearing at a carcass? It wasn't Marcello; it wasn't Tony; it was Nacho. He was responsible for his anger and rage. He owned it. He was the man who was damned. For the first time in his life, he realized he was powerless. He had no power over anything in his life in those walls around him. Hell, what power did he ever have? Even as a kid, decisions were made for him whether he liked them or not. The times he thought he made decisions were simply a delusion. Someone else had told him what to do.

"Damn," he whispered out of fear that someone else would disturb him like JJ had. "But, that is power...power over letting someone else have control of you is nothin more than the power to surrender. I let people tell me what to do, and that is what got me here in the first place. Why, God, why couldn't I have been stronger. Please God, give me a chance, please." Tears began to well up in Nacho's eyes, and he swallowed the urge to cry. In doing so, his throat felt like it had a thick lump in it.

"Isn't there supposed to be some reason for me being me? Mom used to say there was a reason for me , she wouldn't lie," Nacho thought to himself. "'God makes all of us for a purpose', she told me that," Nacho remembered. What meaning was there here? "God, do you have a reason for me being here? I'm sorry I murdered that man. God, I don't even remember it happening. It is like it is erased from my mind. Please, Lord, erase it from my life and make me clean. I'm sorry I let someone else have power over my life, when I should've let you have control over my life. You're the only one who makes decisions better than I can. I just keep screwing things up, God."

Nacho's tears began to surge forward, now, as he realized that the only one who he should give himself over to completely was God. "God doesn't make mistakes, Nacho, He shows us opportunities when WE make the mistakes." His mother's advice came back to him. Yet, life had no meaning while he was locked up, especially in a place where there were no rules. Even the people who supposed to maintain the rules didn't really follow any rules. The guards were simply trying to keep peace, but in doing so they abused their power. It was their kind of peace- keeping a lid on things and mindlessly going through the motions of keeping order in a place where there was little order. Not like things were chaotic, just always the same. As long as you stayed out of their way, they left you alone. You do what they say, and things are okay. Nacho remembered the fly he'd killed when he was a kid when he'd smashed it with his toe until there was nothing left. He, and the others in there, were like the fly. They'd get smashed into nothing if they bothered the guards. Nacho had no power, no meaning, and nothing to hold onto. None of the men did in there. Day after day, the same things happened on schedule. Even though they are all together in there, all those men who were locked up, every man was alone- isolated. They couldn't trust anyone else, not even their 'homes'. They were alone in a crowd of other alone people- alone behind walls made of stone and metal meant to keep them away from people who had each other, life, happiness, and freedom. How can a man get to even know himself here? No room to even stretch out physically how could one stretch out mentally or spiritually? The routine was killing him from the inside. Nacho realized there had to be more- there must be more. The place was destroying him as a man.

As chow time drew near, he knew he had to go into the hall and eat with the rest of the men. Spaghetti, again. As Nacho's plate was filled, he looked around for a table where he would be safe. Off in a corner, he could see Pecas sitting with his back to the group. Nacho made his way over and sat down heavily in the chair.

"You okay?," asked Pecas.

"Yeah, man, I'm okay. Sorry about earlier. I just had..."

Before he could complete the sentence, Pecas interuppted him.
"No, Nacho, don't apologize. I know this place gets to you. It gets to me, too. I get a sick feeling inside when I think my life is here. It's

like..I dunno...I guess the word is 'dead end'. I'm tired, Nacho, I'm tired of this place. I'm tired of the people and tired of being tired."

"Hey, buddy, you got to reach down inside and pull up the strength God gave you."

Pecas stared at nacho for a moment in disbelief. "God? Is God here, Nacho? If he is, I ain't seen him around. If you see him, tell him I'm sorry."

"You can do that yourself, Pecas. Just talk to him."

"Whoa! You went and got some religion! You sounding like J.J., Nacho," Pecas chuckled.

"No, religion found me. God found me, Pecas. I was raised to be believing in God, but things got kinda messed up somewhere along the way."

Just then, Jorge walked up with his tray. Tony was with him. Nacho felt a sick feeling in his stomach, and wanted to get up and walk away. He couldn't, though. That would be disrespecting Jorge who, obviously, had power. Tony took a seat next to Jorge. Pecas was quiet. He didn't look up and kept eating his spaghetti.

"What's up, Nacho?" Jorge said in a deep, monotone voice.

"Not much."

"What could be 'up' in this place," Nacho thought to himself. "There isn't any 'up' here."

Nacho looked over at Tony. Their eyes met only briefly, then Tony quickly glanced away. Pecas finished his meal, and got up to leave.

"Yous got someplace to be, Pecas?" asked Jorge.

"No, nowhere special. Just thought I'd go and let you guys have some time together."

"Hmmm. Thanks, man," Jorge responded staring at him.

Tony was fidgeting with his spaghetti, twirling it around on his plate like eating wasn't on his mind. Jorge sat still, looking at Nacho.

"Nacho, I hear you is close to Pecas. That true?"

"Yeah, maybe. I don't know him especially. Why? People I talk to of special interest to you?" Nacho realized his last remark was challenging Jorge, and could be considered disrespectful, so he quickly added, "Is something up?"

Jorge glared at Nacho for a moment, then looked at Tony like he was expecting something.

"Yeah, Nacho. Something's up," Tony said softly. "Word is..."

There was a pause that seemed almost too long.

."... Well, we think Pecas talks too much. He talks to people he shouldn't be talking to. You know what that means."

Nacho knew what that meant, and he didn't want to go there.

"I don't know. He talks to me, and that's about it."

"You ain't listening, Nacho. Pecas is a problem. I want him done. I want you to do it'.

Nacho felt the blood leave his face; his stomach rolled.

"It needs to be done tomorrow. He trusts you."

"Kill Pecas?," Nacho thought.

"Nacho, tomorrow. Did you hear me?,"

Tony asked with a tone of annoyance.

"Yeah, I heard you. Tomorrow."

XIV

Redemption

After chow time, Nacho thought about Tony and Jorge and how they began to represent all that he hated in the life that was his. Pecas had to be killed, or it would be him. The emptiness of his life, the darkness that seemed endless and void of anything significant, filled his mind. His cell was his world-closed in and locked in. If he was to die tonight, it would be a release from what he had to do, and what he had to do he didn't want to do. Thoughts were random, and seemed disconnected somehow. Nothing made sense, just the opposite of the way it should be. "Something makes sense; nothing is no sense. Nonsense. Hmmm. So, for my life to make sense I need something, not nothing. But, what is something? Where is the something I am missing? Why am I missing the something that makes sense in my life? Why do I have the 'nothings' that fill my world?"

"God, why am I made to be nothing? Why is this happening to me? Why is it that some people have a life filled with easy happiness, and I never got it? I don't understand, God. You became nothing, so I could be something didn't you? My mom used to tell me that. You left Heaven and became nothing but a simple man so that I could become something...something new. Now, I am supposed to do something I don't want to do. Please, please see me through this. Jesus, if you can hear me, help me. I have been a soldier of the streets, now I want to be a soldier for you. Give me a chance, please, give me chance. Let me find some peace. Let me have a way out of this. Let me know you're there for me. I am nothing without you, Jesus." Nacho realized the tears had filled his eyes, and were running down his face.

"Jesus, I have been so filled with hate all my life. I'm sorry for that. I forgive my father. I forgive everyone who has done wrong to me. I need to. If you're going to forgive me, I need to start forgiving others. I forgive them. I want a new life. I'll follow you, now. You'll see. I will follow you, I promise. Guide me. Guide me to do what you want me to do for you. Help me, Jesus. Fill my heart, fill my life, fill all of me with your peace. Jesus, save me!"

As he settled back on his cot, he continued to pray until sleep overcame him.

The next morning, he got into line for breakfast. Something was up; there was something different. Where was Pecas? Nacho looked around, but couldn't see him. One of the other homeboys, got in line behind Nacho.

"Dude, you hear about Pecas?"

"No, esse, what?"

"Last night, man, last night he got shanked. Yeah, some Vato from another gang shanked him right in the throat, man. He's in the hospital. Somone told me they'll move him out to another facility. He's in pretty bad shape. They just missed his artery."

"They know who the Esse was who did this?"

"Yeah, about three cells down from you. The guards don't know, though."

"Thanks, man."

Nacho picked up his breakfast and sat down at his usual table. Jorge and Tony came walking over and sat down.

"Heard about Pecas?"

"Yeah," answered Nacho

"Shame, man."

Nacho got up from the table. He didn't want to talk. He wanted some peace.

Tony grabbed Nacho's shirt, and pulled him in close. "Nacho. Today, we gonna show those Esse's something. You're off the hook with Pecas, but they aren't going to get away with doing that to one of ours. You're going to kick off a riot. You understand? In the yard, today. Then you take that Vato out."

"Yeah," Nacho replied.

He was sick of this, and wanted to go to his cell. When he got back to his cell, two guards came walking up.

"Pizano. C'mon. We need you down in the room."

Nacho walked in front of the guards. "What's up now?"

"You'll find out."

Walking into the room, there was a man dressed in a suit. He was seated at a table with a stack of papers in front of him.

"Mr. Pizano?"

"Yes"

"Mr. Pizano, your mother is here to see you. You can enter into the regular visiting area."

"Really? When"

"Now. Mr. Pizano, improve the behavior."

"Great. I get to visit my mom and then kick off a riot. What is this? Man," he thought.

Nacho walked down to the visitation hall, and his mother was sitting with her back to him. She was expecting to see him behind the glass. He crept up behind her and gave her a hug.

"Oh my, oh my God! Oh, Mico! Mico! This is amazing? Mico!" She stood on her tip toes and hugged him. "Oh, God is great! God is so great! I am so blessed!"

"Mom, I love you! You know that. I love

you so much."

"Mico, I have something for you." His mother handed him a brown folder filled with papers.

"What's this?"

"Mico, read. Read. It is a Writ of habeas corpus. That attorney, you gave an attorney some papers. That started things off, then I went to an attorney but he was ripping me off, so another attorney picked up your case pro bono. Mico, because you were fifteen, you were underage. You aren't supposed to be in here."

Nacho could hardly believe it. He would be transferred out? After the visit, he was walking back to his cell. Then, he remembered. He was supposed to kick off a riot?

He thought, "What kinda sick joke is this, God?"

There was a lockdown at that moment, and everybody had to return to their cells. One of the homeboys came up quickly behind him.

"Stupid Vato's. They just kicked off a

riot! Can you believe that?"

"Really?"

"Yeah. We're in lockdown for awhile."
Nacho thought about this. "Is this for real? I'm
supposed to kill a friend, but don't. I'm getting
out. I was supposed to kick off a riot, and then,
I don't. What is happening? God, is that you?"
Nacho sat in his cell and looked at the walls.
There was so much going on here. What was
the message? Was he supposed to be seeing
something here? Was there a sign?

After the lockdown was lifted, it was time
for lunch. Nacho got into the line for lunch.
The day had been strange, but it seemed to be
getting stranger by the minute.

Lunch was sandwiches and fruit salad.
Nacho grabbed his tray, and went to his table.
It had been an odd morning. He felt someone
coming up behind him. It was Jorge and Tony
again.

"Hey, esse," said Tony

"Hey."

"Things are pretty strange today, eh?"

"Yeah." Nacho wanted to tell Jorge and

Tony about the news, but couldn't.

"So, man, we got that Esse down a few cells from you. He's the one who did Pecas. Remember?"

"Yeah."

"You do him tomorrow."

Nacho hesitated for a moment in responding. He looked at Jorge, who was staring at Nacho with a threatening expression.

"Yeah, yeah. I'll do it," he sighed.

Nacho sat in his cell after lunch. What was going on? This was one crazy day. He took a brief nap, and as he did, he thought back on his life and where he'd been. At every turn, God had been there for him. His mom was right. God would help him again. He felt this deeply in his heart. The storms of his life were taking their toll, but he had to hold on.

"God, one more time, God. One more time. Help me through this. I can't kill that man. I can't. Please God, Please!"

Nacho went to the TV room for awhile, but had a hard time focusing on the screen. There was so much going on. How could he make sense of any of this?

He made his way to the chow line. Meatloaf, canned green beans and instant potatoes were sitting on his plate. He couldn't eat. He felt sick, tired, and worn. Jorge and Tony were at another table, away from Nacho, talking to some other guys. This gave Nacho time to think. How would he do this if he had to? He had to, or else it would be him who would die. Where was the choice? As he got up from the table, he looked over at Tony. Tony, who had killed Jaime, his best friend's brother. How could he have done that? There he was, laughing like nothing had happened.

The walk back to his cell seemed to be a difficult one, and he looked into the cell of the man he was to kill. It was clean and tidy. He went into his cell and sat on his bunk. Depression washed over him. He could hear the sounds of the inmates talking and shouting, the smell of cigarettes filled the air. Gradually, the sounds began to die down as nighttime fell. Nacho settled back on his cot, but couldn't sleep.

Off in the distance, he heard the steps of guards walking down the cell block. They were coming closer, and then they stopped.

"Pack it up. C'mon."

"Yeah, okay."

Something was happening down a couple of cells. Nacho tried to see what was going on. There was movement down at the cell of the man he was to kill. What was going on? He couldn't see. Something was happening.

"You ready?"

"Yeah"

"Is the van ready for L.A?" It was a guard's voice.

Another guard answered, "Yeah, they're just about packed. He's the last one."

The man Nacho was supposed to kill was leaving. It was done.

The next morning, Nacho made a show of it, how he would have done that guy with no remorse, and would have stayed there with his home boys, but in his heart he knew. He knew he was going home. He was going. He would never come back. Never. His life would have to change, and it would take time, but never again would he return to San Quentin.

That day, Nacho was moved out of San Quentin and placed in the C.Y.A. Life was about to begin anew.

Epilogue

Nacho's time in the California Youth Authority gave him time to think about life. He was married at a young age and, within a year, they had a son. It was then that Nacho realized his life had to change. Dictated first by his father, then by the gang relationships he had built, he had no ownership of his life. Others were leading his life for him, and he was paying for them to have the privilege to run his life. He gained nothing; he lost everything. In Nacho's own writing, this is how he described the moment:

> I just got back from the bay area
> my wife at the time had went to vissit
> her sister in the hospital i brought back a
> pound of weed was breaking it down

wen i got the call that my wife just went into labor i was very nervos about haveing a son cuz didnt know if i could love him cuz of the sic relationship i had with my dad i hated my father soo much my mother was the only person alive i truly loved at that time i was married but already having problems so was thinking about leaving her wen i got to the hospital she was already in a room her over bering mother who i had no respect for at the time was already there i angree cuz she felt like she had more right to be there then me so al these amotions are going through my body wen my son was born and i seen him for the first time i sat there just looking at him i could not understand how my father hated me so much wen all i could feel was love for my son OMG it was ammazing to see my son i started crying i didnt even cry wen they let me out of prison i herd him cry for the first time i felt like droping to the floor screeming thank u God i was so over walmed with love and apriciaiton i started thinking how the words and actions of my family led me to the streets how cuz of the way my father was i turned out to be a killing animal..the state of callifornia labeled me a passive but yet agresive psyco pathic maniac ..the city of san jose labeled me a cold blooded killer my family wrote me off as a lost cozz but yet im standing and holding the most beautiful presses sight anybody can amgen i looked my son in his eye and i swore to him he will have a better life then me i told him i will never abondon him i will be the father i always wanted that moment i was no longer a gang banger but i became a father a man .with no regrets i never broke my promise to him or my other son i am the father i dreamed of haveing in my life and my sons still love and respect me....thank u GOD

Today, Nacho is divorced. He raised his two sons on his own. His oldest son is in college. His youngest son, once an active basketball player, was stricken with juvenile arthritis. He lives with Nacho and is a Christian musician. There are days when his son is unable to walk, so Nacho carries him. He carries him with the love of a father; he walks with him in faith. Nacho's basketball team continues to play…and win.